THE KABBALAH

THE KABBALAH

The Religious Philosophy of the Hebrews

By ADOLPHE FRANCK

Translated from the French

CITADEL PRESS
Kensington Publishing Corp.
www.kensingtonbooks.com

CITADEL PRESS books are published by

Kensington Publishing Corp.
850 Third Avenue
New York, NY 10022

All Kensington titles, imprints, and distributed lines are available at special quantity discounts for bulk purchases for sales promotions, premiums, fund raising, educational, or institutional use. Special book excerpts or customized printings can also be created to fit specific needs. For details, write or phone the office of the Kensington special sales manager: Kensington Publishing Corp., 850 Third Avenue, New York, NY 10022, attn: Special Sales Department, phone 1-800-221-2647.

First printing 1987

15 14 13 12 11 10 9 8 7 6 5

Printed in the United States of America

ISBN 0–8065–0708–X

Contents

PART THREE: PHILOSOPHIC RESEMBLANCES TO THE KABBALAH

Introduction

BY JOHN C. WILSON

THIS BOOK IS a faithful translation of one originally written in French and published under the title: La Kabbale; ou la philosophie religieuse des Hébreux, Paris 1843 first edition, second edition 1889, 1892. The author, Adolphe Franck (1809-1893) was a Hebraist and orientalist and published, among other works, a translation of the Pentateuch and a study of mystical philosophers in France centering on St. Martin and his master, Martinez Pasqualis. All this enduring work was, however, his avocation; his living came from filling the chair of professor of natural and legal philosophy at the Collège de France. He produced numerous works in this field as well.

The present book has been shorn of much scholarly apparatus, including footnotes in Hebrew, and a preface examining the previous literature dealing with the origins and meaning of the Kabbalah. Those who wish to consult this scholarly apparatus will find it in the French editions of 1889 and 1892 and in the translation into English by I. Sossnitz published in New York in 1926. The present translation is based on the Sossnitz but has so thoroughly overhauled it that it is, in effect, a new translation. The idea of the present translation is to provide, for the considerable if select audience which is interested in the Kabbalah, the essential text of one of the very few books ever written which aids us in understanding the Kabbalah. As for the tempting but confusing question of origins, suffice it to say that the author—and he has been upheld by later scholarship, including that of the greatest living historian of Jewish mysticism, Professor Gershon Scholem, professor of the history of Jewish mysticism at Hebrew University in Jerusalem—considers the Kabbalah to be pre-Christian and Zoroastrian in origin.

During the hundred years between the original publication of this book and Professor Scholem's work, the Kabbalah underwent almost total eclipse among the Jews of Western Europe. For reasons connected with their entry into Western European life, which became possible only after the French revolution and the spread of religious tolerance, but became possible mainly only if Jews accepted entry as individuals rather than as a mystical community, i.e., as a Frenchman of Jewish faith, a German patriot of the Jewish persuasion, etc. Judaism was oriented in a rationalist, non-mystical direction. The Kabbalah was forgotten, more accurately suppressed as though it were a shameful past.

Franck was one of the very few Jewish philosophers of

his time who, while entering fully into Western European life, sought to preserve and to interpret to the West the ancient wisdom of the Kabbalah. He was able, as this book demonstrates, to show that, far from being the thaumaturgical hugger mugger and nonsense that the Jewish historians characterized it to be, it was an extremely sophisticated and enlightened philosophy, still able after thousands of years to teach advanced civilizations the deeply important distinction between knowledge and wisdom. This book has always in the ensuing hundred years had a devoted hearing from those drawn to the Kabbalah. But it is only now, as an aftermath of the Hitler holocaust, that enlightened Jews are turning with interest to this ancient wisdom in considerable numbers. And with them an audience in the Gentile world, faced with the potential holocaust of the hydrogen bomb.

It is for this new audience that this popular edition of Adolphe Franck's introduction to the Kabbalah is offered.

January 1, 1967

PART ONE

The Kabbalistic Books

CHAPTER ONE

The Antiquity of the Kabbalah

ENTHUSIASTIC partisans of the Kabbalah declare it to have been brought down from heaven by angels to teach the first man, after his fall, how to recover his primal nobility and bliss. Others suppose that the lawgiver of the Hebrews received it directly from God, during his forty days' stay on Mount Sinai, that he transmitted it to seventy old men, sharing with them the gifts of the Holy Spirit, and that they in turn passed it on by word of mouth until the time when Ezra was commanded to transcribe it together with the Law. But the most careful scrutiny of all the books of the Old Testament fails to uncover a single reference to secret teachings or to a doctrine of superior profundity and purity reserved solely for a small number of the elect.

Between the time of their origin and their return from the Babylonian captivity, the Hebrew people, like all infant nations, knew no other agents of truth, no other ministers to the mind, than the prophet, the priest and the poet. In spite of the difference between them, the last is ordinarily confused with the first; and the priest did not teach, but simply attracted attention through ritual pomp. As for teachers—those who teach religion as if it were a science and substitute the tone of dogma for the language of inspiration—in a word, the theologians—there is no mention of either their names or their existence during the entire period.

It is only at the beginning of the third century before the Christian era that they first appear, under the general name of *Tannaim,* which means "teachers of the tradition"; for it is in the name of this new authority "tradition" that everything not clearly expressed in the Scriptures was then taught. The *Tannaim,* the oldest and most respected of all teachers in Israel, form a long chain the last link of which is Judah the Pious, editor of the *Mishna,* who collected and transmitted to posterity all the utterances of his predecessors. Among them are to be found R. Akiba and Simeon ben Yohai, along with his son and his friends, presumed to be the creators of the oldest monuments of the Kabbalah.

Upon the death of Judah towards the close of the second century of the Christian era, a new generation of teachers starts. They are called *Amaraim* because, pretending to no authority themselves, they only repeated and clarified what they learned from the *Tannaim,* making known such of their teachings as had still not been published. These commentaries and new traditions, which multiplied prodigiously for more than three hundred years, were finally collected under the name of *Gemara*—that is to say, the termination and completion of the tradition. It is consequently in these two collections, religiously preserved since their formation to this day and joined together under the name of *Talmud*, that we must primarily search, if not for the very ideas underlying the kabbalistic system, at least for data bearing upon the time and place of its origin.

In the Mishna (*Haggiga*, sec. 2) we find this remarkable passage: "The story of Genesis (the Creation) is not to be explained to two men, the story of the *Merkaba* (Heavenly Chariot) not even to one, unless he be wise and can deduce wisdom of his own accord."

A rabbi of the Talmud, R. Zerah, is still more severe, for he adds that even the chapter headings may be divulged only to men invested with high dignity or known for their extraordinary prudence; or, to translate the original expression literally, "who carry within them a heart full of solicitude."

Evidently, this cannot refer either to the text of Genesis or of Ezekiel, where the prophet tells of his vision of the heavenly chariot on the banks of the river Hebar. The entire Scriptures were, so to speak, on everyone's lips; from time immemorial it has been the duty of scrupulous observers of the tradition to read the Scriptures through in their temples at least once during the year. Moses himself unremittingly advised the study of the Law, universally understood to be the Pentateuch, and after the return from the Babylonian captivity, Ezra read it aloud before the assembled people (Ezra 2:8). Nor is it possible that the words quoted were intended to interdict interpretations of the story of the Creation or the chapter of Ezekiel which would make them comprehensible. At issue is an interpretation, or rather a doctrine which, although known, was taught under the seal of mystery; of a science no less fixed in form than in principles, as evidenced by its division into several chapters each one of which is prefaced by a summary.

It cannot apply to Ezekiel's vision because that occupies not several chapters but only one, and precisely the first. It can be seen, furthermore, that the secret doctrine comprised two parts, which are not accorded equal importance; for one part may not be taught to two persons, while the other may never be entirely divulged, even to one, though he satisfy the severest conditions. If we are to believe Maimonides—who, although a stranger to the Kabbalah, could not deny its existence—the first half, entitled "The Story of Genesis," taught the science of nature, and the second half, called "The Story of the Chariot," contained a treatise on theology. This opinion was accepted by all the Kabbalists.

In order to be initiated into this mysterious and sacred science it was necessary to be distinguished not only by intelligence and eminent position, but by advanced age, as well. Even when these conditions (observed, as well, by modern Kabbalists) were fulfilled, one was not always sure enough of his intelligence or moral strength to accept the burden of these formidable secrets, which might be dangerous to one's belief and the observance of religious law.

A curious example of this is found in the Talmud itself, in allegorical language which is later explained:

> The teachers taught: Four [persons] entered the Garden of Delight, namely: ben Azai, ben Zoma, Aher and R. Akiba. Ben Azai looked around and died. To him may

> be applied the verse of the Scriptures: 'Precious in the sight of the Lord is the death of His saints' [Ps. 116:15]. Ben Zoma also looked around and lost his reason. The Scriptures say of [such as] him: 'Hast thou found honey, eat so much as is sufficient for thee, lest thou be filled therewith and vomit it' [Prov. 25:16]. Aher made ravages in the plantations. Akiba entered in peace and came out in peace.

It is hardly possible to take this passage literally and to suppose that it refers to a material vision of the splendors of another life; for the Talmud never uses the purely mystical terms of the text quoted when speaking of Paradise. And how can we admit that a man could lose either faith or reason, as did two of the persons in this legend, after seeing during his lifetime the heavenly powers awaiting the elect? We must, therefore, agree with the most reputable Jewish authorities that the Garden of Delight entered by the four masters is nothing but the mysterious science mentioned above—a science dangerous to weak intelligences because it may lead either to insanity or to deviations more fatal than impiety. It is to the latter consequence that the Gemara points when it says of Aher, so famous in Talmudic narrations, that he "made ravages in the plantations." According to the Gemara, Aher (whose real name was Elisha ben Abua) had been one of the wisest teachers in Israel. His name was changed to Aher (which literally means "another"—that is, another man) to indicate the alteration he had undergone. And, in fact, when he came out of the allegorical garden into which his fatal curiosity had led him, he became an open infidel. He abandoned himself, says the text, to the generation of evil, threw over morality, betrayed his faith, led a scandalous life, and was even taxed with the murder of a child. Where, really, was his error? Whither had his researches into the most important secrets of religion led him? The Jerusalem Talmud plainly states that Aher recognized two supreme principles. The Babylonian Talmud, the source of this entire story, gives us to understand the same thing, informing us that when Aher saw in heaven the power of Metatron, the angel next to God, he exclaimed: "Perhaps there are two supreme powers."

We need not dwell too long upon this fact for we must cite others, more significant; yet, it is noteworthy that the angel, or rather the hypostasis called Metatron, plays a very great part in the kabbalistic system. It is he, properly speaking, who governs this visible world; he reigns over all the spheres suspended in space, over all the planets and celestial bodies, as well as over all the angels who control them; for above him is nothing but the intelligible forms of the Divine Essence and spirits so pure that they cannot exercise any immediate control over material things. Also, it has been found that the numerical value of his name is equal to that of the synonym of the Almighty.

The Kabbalah is undoubtedly, as we shall soon prove, much further removed from dualism than from monism; yet does not its allegorical separation of the intelligible essence of God from the ruling power of the world explain the heresy described in the Gemara?

A final citation from the same source, and accompanied by Maimonides' reflections, will complete the demonstration of our main point: that a kind of philosophy, a religious metaphysics, in a manner of speaking, was taught by word of mouth among some of the Tannaim, the earliest theologians of Judaism. The Talmud tells us that in ancient times three names were known to express the idea of God: the famous Tetragrammaton, or name of four letters, and two names foreign to the Bible, the first of which consisted of twelve letters, the other of forty-two. The first, though forbidden to the masses, circulated freely enough within the schools. "The wise men," the text says, "taught it once a week to their sons and their disciples."

The twelve-lettered name was originally still more widely disseminated. "It was imparted to everybody. But when the number of the impious multiplied, it was confined only to the most discreet of the priests, and they had to recite it under their breath to their brethren during the benediction." Finally, the name composed of forty-two letters was looked upon as the most holy of the mysteries. "It was taught only to one who was considered discreet, of ripe age, neither violent of temper, nor immoderate, nor stubborn, and gentle in his associations." "He who has been instructed in this secret," adds the Talmud, "and guards it with vigilance and a pure heart, may count on the love of God and on the favor of men; his name inspires respect, his knowledge is protected against oblivion, and he is heir to two worlds—the world we live in and the world to come."

Maimonides aptly remarks that there is no name composed of forty-two letters in any language, and certainly not in Hebrew, where vowels are not part of the alphabet. He concludes that the forty-two letters formed several words, each expressing a definite idea or fundamental attribute to the Supreme Being, and all together providing the true definition of the Divine Essence. When it is said, then, that this name embraced a study in itself, knowledge of which was entrusted to only the wisest, it undoubtedly means, continues Maimonides, that in order to define the essence of God, His uniqueness and that of things in general would either have to be better elucidated or further developed. This is surely also the case with the four-lettered name; for, how is it possible to suppose that a name so frequently encountered in the Bible, and to which the Bible itself gives the sublime definition, "*ego sum qui sum,*" had been kept a secret whispered once a week by the wise men into the ears of a few chosen disciples? What the Talmud calls knowledge of the names of God, concludes Maimonides, is but a small part of theology or metaphysics. That is why it was said to be proof against oblivion; for oblivion is not possible to ideas which have their seat in the active intelligence, that is, in reason.

It would be difficult to reject these reflections, recommended no less by the common sense of the free thinker than by profound science and the generally recognized authority of the Talmudists. We add here one further observation, perhaps of very questionable importance in the commonsense view, but of value to the system of ideas on which these researches bear, and a historical fact: Counting all the letters of the sacramental Hebrew names, the names of the ten Sefiroth of the Kabbalah, and prefixing the last with the conjunctive particle "v", we obtain precisely the number 42. Could this not be the thrice holy name so tremblingly confined even to the elite? Here is full justification for all of Maimonides' comments.

To begin with, these forty-two letters really form not one name but several words. Then, each of these words expresses, in the opinion of the Kabbalists at least, an essential attribute of the Divinity, or—what is the same thing to them—one of the necessary forms of existence. Finally, all together, these words represent—according to the kabbalistic science and to the *Zohar* and its commentators—the most exact definition of the supreme principle of all things that our minds are capable of conceiving. Given such a concept of God, separated as it is by an abyss from common belief, it is very easy to appreciate all the precautions taken to confine it to the circle of initiates. For the time being we shall not insist on this point, whose importance we in no way exaggerate; we are satisfied to have exhibited the evidence, which emerges from the passages quoted.

At the time, then, when the Mishna was edited, there existed a secret doctrine concerning the Creation and Divine Nature. There was agreement on the manner of its study and division, and its name excited a kind of religious awe even among those who could not have known it. But how long had this doctrine existed? And if we cannot determine that precisely, is there any way of telling when the deep shadows formed that shrouded its origin? This is the question which we shall now attempt to answer.

In the opinion of the most reliable historians, the editing of the Mishna came to an end no later than the year 3949 after Creation, 189 years after the birth of Christ. Bearing in mind that Judah the Holy merely collected the precepts and traditions transmitted to him by his predecessors, the Tannaim, it must be concluded that the quotations forbidding imprudent disclosure of the Creation and of the Merkaba are, consequently, older than the book that contains them. True, we do not know the author of these words. But this in itself is further proof of their antiquity; for, had they expressed the opinion of only one man, they would not have been invested with legislative power and, as is usual under such circumstances, the responsible person would have been named.

Besides, the doctrine itself necessarily preceded the law that forbids its disclosure. It must have been known and must have acquired a certain authority before the danger of its dissemination among the doctors and masters of Israel, as well as the people, was recognized. So, without undue boldness, we may date it, at the latest, from the end of the first century of the Christian era. This is precisely the time when Akiba and Simeon ben Yohai lived, to whom the Kabbalists attribute the composition of their most important and most celebrated works. The same generation also included R. Jose of Zippora, whom the *Idra Rabba*—an ancient and remarkable fragment of the *Zohar*—lists among the intimate friends and most fervent disciples of Simeon ben Yohai. It is evidently to him that the talmudic treatise from which we have drawn most of our citations attributes a knowledge of the holy Merkaba.

Among the authorities testifying to the antiquity, at least of the kabbalistic ideas if not of the books, is the Chaldaic translation of the Five Books of Moses by Onkelos. This famous translation was looked upon with such great respect that it was regarded as a divine revelation. It is assumed by the Babylonian Talmud that Moses received it on Mount Sinai when he received the written and oral Law, that it came down to the time of the Tannaim by tradition, and that Onkelos had only the glory of transcribing it. A great many modern theologians believe the foundations of Christianity are to be found in Onkelos. They especially claim to recognize the second divine person in the word *Memra,* which actually means "word" or "thought," and which the translator has substituted everywhere for the name of Jehovah.

This much is certain, that the spirit of the translation contradicts that of the Mishna, the Talmud, normative

Judaism and the Pentateuch itself; in short, it contains many traces of mysticism. Wherever it is possible or important, an idea is substituted for a fact or an image, literal meaning is sacrificed to spiritual meaning, and anthropomorphism is excised in the interest of describing the divine attributes.

In an age when the worship of the dead letter deteriorated into idolatry, when men passed their lives in counting the verses, the words and the letters of the Law, the official preceptors, the legitimate representatives of religion, found nothing better to do than to crush the intellect as well as the will under an increasing mass of extraneous rituals. This aversion to all material and practical considerations, coupled with the habit of sacrificing grammar and history in the interest of an exalted idealism, unmistakably lays bare the existence of a secret doctrine having all the characteristics and claims of mysticism and undoubtedly dating to a much earlier period. Finally, in order to attain their aims and to introduce their own ideas into the very terms of the revelation, the Kabbalists resorted at times to more or less irrational means. One such means was to form a new alphabet by changing the value of the letters, or better, by substituting one letter for another according to a definite plan. This method is frequently employed in the Talmud, as well as in a translation older than Onkelos—the Aramaic paraphrase by Jonathan ben Uzziel, contemporary and disciple of Hillel the Aged, who taught with great authority during the early years of the reign of Herod.

To be sure, such procedures may equivocally serve the most diverse ideas; but men do not invent an artificial language and deliberately withhold its keys unless they have resolved to hide their thoughts at least from the masses. Moreover, although the Talmud makes frequent use of similar methods, it does not employ the one we have described and which we believe to be the oldest. Taken separately, this fact would have little demonstrative value, but added to those described above, it is not to be disregarded. Taken together and comparatively, we are justified in stating that before the end of the first century of the Christian era, there circulated among the Jews a profoundly venerated science which could be distinguished from the Mishna, the Talmud and the Sacred Books—a mystic doctrine evidently engendered by the need for reflection and independence as well as philosophy; and which, nevertheless, invoked in its favor the united authority of tradition and Scriptures.

The guardians of this doctrine, whom we henceforth shall not hesitate to call Kabbalists, should not and cannot be confused with the Essenes, known from a much earlier epoch but persisting in customs and beliefs until some time after the reign of Justinian. In fact, if we refer to Josephus and Philo, the only authors deserving confidence on this point, the aim of this famous sect was essentially moral and practical; it endeavored to inculcate the kind of equality and fraternity which was later so brilliantly expounded by the founder and the apostles of Christianity. The Kabbalah, on the other hand, according to the oldest testimony was entirely a speculative science, which claimed to unveil the secrets of the Creation and of Divine Nature.

The Essenes were an organized society very similar to the religious communities of the Middle Ages. Their way of life reflected their feelings and their ideas; moreover, they admitted into their midst all those who distinguished themselves by a pure life, even women and children. The Kabbalists always shrouded themselves in mystery from their first appearance to the time when the press betrayed their secret. At rare intervals and after many precautions, they half-opened their portals for some new adept, always chosen exclusively from among the intellectual elite and from among those whose advanced age promised discretion and wisdom.

Finally, in spite of their all too pharisaical observance of the Sabbath, the Essenes were certainly not afraid publicly to reject the traditions and to accord morality a conspicuous preference over cult; they even went so far as to reject both the sacrifices and the ceremonies commanded by the Pentateuch. Like most Christian mystics and like the Karmathians among the followers of Islam, the adepts of the Kabbalah, for their part, adhered to all the ritual practices; they were generally careful not to attack the tradition, which they themselves invoked. As we have already noted, several of them were among the most revered doctors of the Mishna. We might add that thereafter they rarely abandoned their prudent habits.

CHAPTER TWO

The Authenticity of the Sefer Yetzirah

WE COME now to the original books on the basis of which, in most opinions, the kabbalistic system was initially formulated. Judging from the titles which come down to us, there were a great number of such works, but we shall consider only those which have been preserved and commend themselves to our attention as much by their importance as by their antiquity. Two such books fully correspond with the Talmud's conception of the Story of Genesis and the Holy Merkaba. One, entitled the "Book of Formation" (*Sefer Yetzirah*), contains, if not a system of physics, at least a kind of cosmology, conceivable in an epoch and country where the habit of explaining all phenomena as the immediate effect of the first cause must have stifled the spirit of inquiry. Consequently, certain general and superficial relations perceived in the external world must have passed for the science of nature. The other book is called the *Zohar* meaning "brightness," a title derived from the verse in Daniel: "And they that be wise shall shine as the brightness of the firmament." It deals more particularly with God, with the spirits and with the human soul—in a word, with the spiritual world. These two books are certainly not comparable in value and importance. The *Zohar*, much richer and more comprehensive, but also abounding with difficulties, is the more important; the *Sefer Yetzirah* the more ancient.

Talmudic texts, neither the meaning nor age of which have been established, have been invoked to prove the antiquity of the *Sefer Yetzirah*. We shall ignore these as well as the legends and controversies to which they have given rise and limit our observations to the chief features of the book. These will suffice for an appreciation of its character and lofty origin.

1. The system it contains corresponds in every respect to the idea conveyed by its title. We are so assured by its first proposition: "With thirty-two marvelous paths of wisdom the world was created by the Eternal, the Lord of Hosts, the God of Israel, the Living, the Almighty, the Supreme God Who dwells in Eternity, Whose name is sublime and holy."

2. Its method of explaining the work of Creation and the importance it attaches to numbers and letters are instructive for an understanding of how this principle was later abused by ignorance and superstition; how the fables we have mentioned spread and finally how the so-called

practical Kabbalah, which endows numbers and letters with the power to change the course of nature, took shape.

The form is simple and dignified; nothing with the faintest resemblance to demonstration or argument; only aphorisms, regularly distributed, but each as concise as the ancient oracles. One striking fact is that the term later used exclusively to specify the soul is still used here, as it is in the Pentateuch and throughout the Old Testament, to designate the living human body.

There are many words of foreign origin in the book: the names of the seven planets and of the Celestial Dragon, mentioned several times, evidently are part of the language as well as the science of the Chaldeans, who exercised an all-powerful influence over the Hebrews during the Babylonian captivity. But the purely Greek, Latin and Arabic expressions, frequently employed in the Talmud and in more modern Hebrew writings dealing with philosophy and science, are not found in *Sefer Yetzirah.*

As a general rule and, I dare say, an infallible one, all works of this nature, in which neither the Greek nor the Arab civilizations have a part, can be considered to antedate the birth of Christianity. It must be acknowledged, however, that vestiges of the language and philosophy of Aristotle are to be found in the work under consideration which we do not hesitate to characterize as pre-Christian.

After stating its first proposition, *Sefer Yetzirah* adds that there are three terms: that which counts, that which is counted, and the very act of counting—translated by the oldest commentators as: the subject, the object, and the act of reflection or thought. It is impossible not to recall in this the celebrated phrase of the twelfth book of Aristotle's *Metaphysics*: the intelligence comprehends itself by grasping the intelligible, and it becomes the intelligible by the very act of comprehension and cognition; hence, the intelligence and the intelligible are identical. But it is evident that the three terms are a later addition to the text, for they are connected neither with the proposition which precedes them nor the one that follows. They do not recur in any other part of the book, whereas the use of the ten numbers and twenty-two letters, which form the thirty-two means applied to Creation by Divine Wisdom, is explained at great length. Finally, it is hard to understand why these terms should be found in a treatise whose sole concern is with the relations that exist between the various parts of the material world.

The difference between the two manuscripts reproduced in the Mantua edition, one at the end of the volume, the other amidst the diverse commentaries, are far from being as great as certain critics would have us believe. An impartial and detailed comparison shows that the manuscripts differ only in some unimportant variants such as may be encountered in all ancient works which, by virtue of their very antiquity, have suffered in the course of centuries from the inattention and ignorance of copiers and the temerity of commentators. In fact, both manuscripts rest on the same foundation and expound the same general system; they are even divided in the same way and have the same number of chapters, presented in the same order to the same subject matter. What is more, the same ideas are expressed in the same terms. What we do not find is a perfect correspondence in the numbers and placement of the diverse propositions. One manuscript has repetitions, the other abbreviations; one combines what the other separates; and, lastly, one appears to be more explicit than the other, both in words and meaning.

We know of only one passage where the last difference

is visible. At the end of the first chapter, where the principles of the universe which correspond to the ten numbers are enumerated, one manuscript simply says that first of all comes the spirit of the Living God; the other adds that this spirit of the Living God is the Holy Spirit which is at the same time Spirit, Voice and World. Doubtless this idea is of the greatest importance but it is not missing from the less explicit manuscript, either. It is, as we shall soon prove, the basis for, and the consequence of, the entire system. Moreover, the "Book of Formation" was translated and explained in Arabic at the commencement of the tenth century by Rabbi Saadia, a man with a lofty, methodical and wise mind, who considered it one of the principal and most ancient monuments of the human intelligence. Without allowing this testimony undue credit, it should be noted that the commentators who succeeded Saadia during the twelfth and thirteenth centuries expressed the same conviction.

Like all ancient works, *Sefer Yetzirah* lacks a title and author's name, but it closes with these strange words:

> And when the patriarch Abraham had considered, examined, fathomed and grasped the meaning of all these things, the Master of the Universe manifested Himself to him, called him His friend, and entered into an eternal covenant with him and his posterity. Abraham then believed in God, and that was reckoned unto him as an act of justice; and the glory of God was called upon him; for it is to Abraham that the verse applies: 'I have known thee before I formed thee in the womb of thy mother.'

This passage cannot be construed as a modern invention. With slight alterations it exists in both texts of the Mantua edition and is to be found in the oldest commentaries.

It is our opinion that in order to heighten interest in the "Book of Formation," its authors claimed that it contained exactly the same observations as were made by the first patriarch of the Hebrews and which gave him the idea of a God, One and All-Powerful.

Abraham himself has been taken to be the author of the book in which his name is mentioned with religious respect. Moses Botril's commentary on the *Sefer Yetzirah* begins thus:

> It was Abraham, our father [peace be upon him!], who wrote this book against the wise men of his time who were incredulous of the principles of monotheism. At least that is what R. Saadia [the memory of the just be blessed!] claims in the first chapter of his book 'The Philosopher's Stone.' In his own words: 'The wise men of Chaldea attacked Abraham, our father, for his belief. Now, the sages of Chaldea were divided into three sects. The first sect claimed that the universe was subject to two primal conflicting causes, one of which was busy destroying what the other produced. This opinion corresponds with that of the dualists, who rest their theory on the principle that there can be nothing in common between the Author of good and the author of evil. Since these two contrary principles reciprocally paralyze each other, and as nothing can be accomplished in this manner, the second sect recognized a third, deciding, principle. The third sect, finally, confessed no other God but the sun, which it recognized as the sole principle of life and death.'

Notwithstanding the imposing and universally respected authority of Saadia, this view has no adherents nowadays. The name of the patriarch has long since been replaced by that of Akiba, one of the most fanatical champions of the tradition and a martyr to his country's liberty, who would have been numbered by posterity among the most admirable heroes had he played a part in the ancient republics of Athens and Rome.

Akiba is less improbable as the author of *Sefer Yetzirah* than Abraham; yet we believe this theory to be equally baseless. Although the Talmud everywhere represents Akiba as an almost divine being, ranking him even above Moses, he is nowhere presented as one of the luminaries of the Merkaba or of the science of Genesis; nowhere are we led to surmise that he wrote the "Book of Formation" or any other book of that nature. On the contrary, he was positively reproached for not having held very lofty ideas on the nature of God. "How long, Rabbi Akiba," said Rabbi Jose the Galilean to him, "how long will you continue to profane the Divine Majesty?" The enthusiasm he inspired resulted from the importance he accorded to the tradition and the diligence with which he extracted from it rules for all actions of life, by the zeal with which he taught during a period of forty years, and also, perhaps, by the heroism of his death. The twenty-four thousand disciples attributed to Akiba do not sit well with the Mishna's ban on divulging even the least important secrets of the Kabbalah to more than one person.

Several modern critics have fancied that there were two different works under the same title, *Sefer Yetzirah*, one of which, attributed to the patriarch Abraham, having long since disappeared, while the other, much more modern, was preserved. This opinion is founded on gross ignorance. Morinus borrowed it from a chronicler of the sixteenth century who, speaking of Akiba, said: "Akiba is he who composed the 'Book of Formation,' in honor of the Kabbalah; but there is another 'Book of Formation' composed by Abraham, to which Rabbi Moses ben Nahman wrote a great and marvelous commentary."

This commentary, written at the close of the thirteenth century but printed in the Mantua edition several years after the above-mentioned chronicle, evidently relates to the book now in our hands. It faithfully preserves the expressions of the text, and it is evident that it was not read by the sixteenth-century historian. Besides, the first to name Akiba as Abraham's successor in composing *Sefer Yetzirah* was a Kabbalist of the fourteenth century, Isaac de Lattes. In his preface to the *Zohar*, he asked: "Who permitted Rabbi Akiba to write the book which has been orally transmitted since Abraham?" This question evidently assumes that there is only one *Sefer Yetzirah*. So the author of the "Book of Formation" is as yet undiscovered; nor is it we who are to rend the veil which hides his name. We even doubt whether that is possible with the feeble means at our disposal. But the uncertainty on this point to which we are condemned does not by any means extend to the propositions we have demonstrated and which can be sufficient for a purely philosophical inquiry.

CHAPTER THREE

The Authenticity of the Zohar

MUCH MORE interesting but also far more difficult is the *Zohar,* or the "Book of Brightness," the universal code of the Kabbalah. Taking the modest form of a commentary on the Pentateuch, it touches with absolute independence on all questions of a spiritual nature, rising at times to the height of doctrines which even the strongest intellect of our day might be proud of. But it rarely maintains the heights, often sinking to language, sentiments and ideas that betray the utmost ignorance and superstition. Side by side with the virile simplicity and naive enthusiasm of biblical times, we find names, facts, reports and habits that take us directly into the Middle Ages.

This unevenness of form as of thought; this fantastic mixture of characteristics from very widely separated times, and finally the almost absolute silence of the two Talmuds in regard to the *Zohar* and the lack of positive documents until the close of the thirteenth century—all have given rise to the most divergent opinions on the origin and author of this book.

All that has been said of the composition and antiquity of the *Zohar* is summed up impartially by two authors. Abraham ben Solomon Zacuto, in his *Sefer Yuhasin* ("Book of Genealogies"), states:

> The *Zohar,* whose rays illumine the world, and which contains the most profound mysteries of the Law and of the Kabbalah, is not the work of Simeon ben Yohai, although it was published under his name. Based on his words, it was edited by his disciples; they in turn entrusted the continuation of their task to other disciples. Written by men who had lived long enough to know the Mishna and all the opinions and precepts of the oral law, the *Zohar* is consequently in harmony with truth. The book was not discovered until after the deaths of Rabbi Moses ben Nahman and Rabbi Asher, who knew of it.

Rabbi Gedalia, author of the famous chronicle "The Chain of Tradition," declares:

> Around the year five thousand and fifty of the Creation (1290 C. E.), various persons claimed that all parts of the *Zohar* written in the Jerusalem dialect [the Aramaic dialect] were composed by Rabbi Simeon ben Yohai, but all those parts written in the sacred language [Hebrew] ought not to be attributed to him. Others affirmed that Rabbi Moses ben Nahman, having discovered the book

> in the Holy Land, sent it to Catalonia, whence it passed to Aragon and fell into the hands of Moses de Leon. Finally, there were those who thought that Moses de Leon, a learned man, had invented all these commentaries and published them under the name of Rabbi Simeon ben Yohai and his friends, to derive profit from scholars. It is added that he acted thus because he was poor and crushed by burdens. . . . As far as I am concerned, I hold that all these opinions are baseless. I believe, to the contrary, that Rabbi Simeon ben Yohai and his pious association did really say all these things and many more. It may be that they were not properly collated at the time. After a long time the separate portions were collected and put in order. This is not surprising, for it was thus that our master, Judah the Pious, edited the Mishna, the different manuscripts of which were at first scattered to the four corners of the earth. In like manner, Rabbi Ashi collected the Gemara.

In short, there are three answers to the question of authorship. Some scholars maintain that, barring a few passages written in Hebrew—which do not exist nowadays in any edition or in any known manuscript—the *Zohar* is to be ascribed entirely to Simeon ben Yohai; others attribute it to an impostor called Moses de Leon, and date it no earlier than the end of the thirteenth or the beginning of the fourteenth century; still other scholars have endeavored to reconcile these two extreme opinions by supposing that Simeon ben Yohai was content to propagate his doctrine through oral teachings, and that his words, preserved either in the minds or in the notebooks of his disciples, were not collated until several centuries after his death, as the book of the *Zohar*.

The first theory, taken literally, is hardly worthy of serious refutation. Let us first look at the fact which was to serve as its basis and which we shall borrow from the Talmud:

> Rabbi Judah, Rabbi Jose and Rabbi Simeon were together one day; a certain Judah ben Gerim stood nearby. Rabbi Judah opened [the conversation] and said: 'How beautiful are the works of this nation [Rome]; they have built bridges, markets and public baths!' Rabbi Jose kept silence, but Rabbi Simeon ben Yohai answered: 'Whatever they built, they built it in their own interest. They built markets to attract prostitutes; they built baths for their own pleasure, and they built bridges to levy taxes on.' Judah ben Gerim went out and told what he had heard. The news reached the ears of Caesar [the Roman government]. The latter rendered the following judgment: 'Judah, who exalted the Roman government, shall be raised in dignity; Jose, who kept silence, shall be exiled to Cyprus; Simeon, who spoke ill of the government, shall be put to death.' Accompanied by his son, Rabbi Simeon immediately repaired to the house of study, whither his wife brought him daily a loaf of bread and a bowl of water. But when the proscriptive decree became too oppressive, he said to his son: 'Woman is light-minded, and, if tortured, your mother may betray us.' So they left and hid in a deep cave.
>
> There, by a miracle, a St. John's bread tree and a spring of water were provided them. Simeon and his son stripped and, buried to their necks in sand, passed all day meditating upon the Law. Twelve years they spent in the cave, until the prophet Elijah came, stood at the entrance of the cave, and exclaimed: 'Who will announce to the son of Yohai that Caesar is dead, and that the proscription has been revoked?' They went forth and saw people sowing and plowing.

There is a tradition (one not vouched for by the Talmud) that during these twelve years of solitude and proscription, Simeon ben Yohai, aided by his son Eleazar, composed the renowned work to which his name is still affixed. Even if we were to strip this tale of its legendary elements, it would still be difficult to justify this inference. For we are not enlightened as to the object or results of the meditations in which the two proscripts tried to forget their suffering. Besides, there are a great many facts and names in the *Zohar* which Simeon ben Yohai, who died a few years after the destruction of Jerusalem in the second century of the Christian era, could certainly not have known. For instance, how could he have spoken of the six portions into which the Mishna is divided, when it was written nearly sixty years after his death? How could he have described the authors and the dialect of the Gemara, when it commences at the death of Judah the Saint and does not end until five hundred years after the birth of Christ? How could he have learned the names of vowel signs and other innovations by the school of Tiberias, when that school could not have come into existence earlier than the beginning of the sixth century?

Several critics have suggested that "Ishmaelites," in the *Zohar*, refers to the Muslim Arabs described in modern Jewish writings. The following passage would seem to make it difficult to deny such an interpretation:

> The moon is at one and the same time the sign of good and the sign of evil. The full moon signifies good, the new moon signifies evil; since it can be either good or evil, the children of Israel and the children of Ishmael have both taken the moon as the object of their calculations. If an eclipse takes place during the full moon, it is not a good omen for Israel; if, on the contrary, the

> eclipse takes place during the new moon [an eclipse of the sun], it is a bad omen for Ishmael. Thus are verified the words of the prophet [Isa. 29:14]: 'The wisdom of their wise men shall perish, and the understanding of their prudent shall be hid.'

But it must be noted that these words are not part of the original *Zohar* text; they were borrowed from a far less ancient commentary entitled "The Faithful Shepherd," which the first editors inserted into the *Zohar* on their own authority, wherever they found a gap.

A passage even more decisive could have been found in the *Zohar,* for this is what a disciple of Simeon ben Yohai purports to have heard from the mouth of his master:

> Woe to the hour when Ishmael was born and invested with the sign of circumcision! For, what did the Lord do, He whose name be blessed? He excluded the children of Ishmael from the celestial union. But since they had merited the sign of the covenant, He reserved for them here below a portion in the Holy Land. The children of Ishmael are, therefore, destined to reign over the Holy Land, and they shall hinder the children of Israel from returning to it. But this condition shall last only until such time as the merit of the children of Ishmael shall be exhausted. They will then excite terrible wars on earth; the children of Edom will unite against them and war upon them, some on land, some on sea, and others near Jerusalem. Victory will rest now with one side, now with the other; but the Holy Land will not be delivered into the hands of the children of Edom.

By Edom, the Jewish writers (that is, those who employed the Hebrew language) designated first pagan

Rome, and next Christian Rome and all ancient peoples in general. As there can be no question here of pagan Rome, the passage doubtless refers to the strife between the Saracens and the Christian crusaders before the fall of Jerusalem. But these facts are now general knowledge and need no repetition. One last observation: to be convinced that Simeon ben Yohai cannot possibly be the sole author of the *Zohar*, and that the book is not the fruit of thirteen years of meditation and solitude, one must study the stories almost always connected with the exposition of the ideas. Thus, in the fragment entitled *Idra Zuta*, an admirable section in the vast kabbalistic compilation, we are told that when near death, Simeon ben Yohai summoned a small number of his disciples and friends, including his son Eleazar, for last instructions.

"Thou," he said to Eleazar, "shalt teach; Rabbi Abba will write, and my other friends will meditate in silence." The master ben Yohai is seldom introduced as speaking. His doctrines are recited by his son or friends, who come together after his death to share the memories of his teachings and to enlighten one another on the common faith. They considered the words of the Scriptures, "How good and how pleasant it is for brethren to dwell together in unity," applicable to themselves. Meeting on the road, their conversation promptly turns upon the habitual subject of their meditations, and some passage of the Old Testament is explained in a purely spiritual sense. Here is one example taken at random out of thousands:

> Rabbi Judah and Rabbi Jose were together on a journey. Rabbi Judah said to his companion: 'Tell me something from the Law, and the Divine Spirit will descend to us; for as often as man meditates upon the words of the Law, the spirit of God either joins him or shows him the way.'

It is quite evident, accordingly, that the author of the *Zohar,* whoever he may have been, did not intend to attribute the book to Simeon ben Yohai, of whose last moments and death he tells us.

Finally, the *Zohar* cites books of which only widely scattered fragments have come down to us; these must necessarily be considered more ancient than the *Zohar* itself. We might believe the following passage to have been written by some disciple of Copernicus, were we not compelled to date it from the end of the thirteenth century at the latest:

> The book of Hamuna the Elder fully explains that the earth turns upon itself like a sphere; that some people are above, others below; that all creatures adapt their appearance to the climate of the region, although always keeping the same position; that certain places on earth are light, while others are in darkness; that some have daylight while others have night, and that there are countries where it is always daylight, or at least, where night lasts but a few moments.

Have we, then, no alternative save to honor an obscure rabbi of the thirteenth century, an unfortunate charlatan who must have devoted long years to composing it in the hope of relieving his penury? Surely not! The secret nature and the intrinsic value of the book make it easy to prove that Moses de Leon was not the author. But we possess arguments still more positive. The *Zohar* is written in an Aramean language of no particular dialect. What scheme could have motivated de Leon to employ an idiom not in use in his time? Was he, as Morinus maintains, trying to lend a semblance of truth to his fictions by having the various persons, under whose names he wished to pass off his own ideas, speak the language of their age? But as a man of great scholarship, de Leon must have known that Simeon ben Yohai and his friends were among the authors of the Mishna; and, although they spoke Jerusalem dialect, it would have been more natural for them to have written in Hebrew.

Some scholars maintain that de Leon really did write in Hebrew, that he did not invent the *Zohar,* but only falsified it by inserting his own opinions, and that his imposture was soon discovered. As no such Hebrew version of the *Zohar* has come down to us, this assertion need not occupy us. Whether true or false, it confirms our observations. Besides, we are quite sure that Moses de Leon wrote a kabbalistic book in Hebrew, which bears the title, "The Name of God," or simply "The Name" (*Sefer ha-Shem*). The work is still in manuscript and was seen by Moses Cordovero. From the few passages he quotes, it is evident that it was a very detailed and frequently very subtle commentary on some of the most obscure points of the doctrine taught in the *Zohar.* For example: What are the different channels, that is to say, the influences and mutual relations, obtaining between all the Sefiroth? Which channels conduct the divine light, or primordial substance of things, from one Sefiroth to another? Is it possible that the same man, who had earlier written the *Zohar* in the Chaldeo-Syriac dialect—whether to add interest by the difficulty of the language, or to make his thoughts inaccessible to the common people—would afterward consider it necessary to explain and develop in Hebrew, for all to understand, mysteries which, at the cost of so much labor and trouble, he had hidden in a language almost forgotten even by scholars? Are we to say that this was still another trick to put his readers on the scent? But this is too much trickery, too much time, patience and effort expended for the miserable aim of which he is accused; the contrivances are too erudite and too complicated for a man who has been accused of both the most stupid contradictions and the grossest anachronisms.

Another reason compels us to view the *Zohar* as a work composed long before the time of Moses de Leon and far removed from Europe. It does not contain the least vestige of the philosophy of Aristotle nor a single mention of Christianity or its founder. But Christianity and Aristotle exercised absolute authority in Europe in the thirteenth and fourteenth centuries. How, then, could a poor Spanish rabbi have written in those fanatical days on religious subjects, without lodging some complaint against Christianity, which the Talmudists and later writers attacked so frequently, and without succumbing, as did Saadia, Maimonides and all the others who pursued the same course, to the inevitable influence of the peripatetic philosophy? In all the commentaries on the "Book of Formation," in all the philosophic and religious monuments of that epoch and of several centuries previous, we find the language of the *Organum* and the influence of the Stagirite.

The absence of this influence is a fact of incontestable importance. We need not look in the Sefiroth for any veiled imitation of Aristotle's categories; for while the latter are but of logical value, the Sefiroth contain a metaphysical system of the highest order. If there are some aspects of resemblance between the Kabbalah and any Greek philosophical system, it is the Platonic. But the same can be claimed for every kind of mysticism; besides, Plato was little known outside his fatherland.

It is to be noted, finally, that the ideas and expressions which are essential and exclusively dedicated to the kabbalistic system, expounded in the *Zohar*, are also found in writings originating much earlier than the close of the thirteenth century. Thus, according to Moses Botril, one of the commentators of the *Sefer Yetzirah*, the doctrine of emanation, as understood by the Kabbalists, was known to Saadia. Botril cites the following words which, he says, are quoted literally from "The Philosopher's Stone" (a work, it is true, wrongly attributed to Saadia):

> O thou man who drawest from the cisterns at the source, guard thyself, when tempted, from revealing anything of the doctrine of emanation, which is a great mystery for all the Kabbalists; and this mystery is hidden in the words of the Law: 'Thou shalt not tempt the Lord.'

Nevertheless, Saadia, in his "Beliefs and Opinions," very forcibly attacks the doctrine which is the basis of the system expounded in the *Zohar* as evidenced in the following passage:

> I have sometimes met men who cannot deny the existence of a Creator, but who think that our mind cannot conceive that something could be made from nothing. Now, as the Creator is the only Being Who was in existence at first, they maintain that He drew everything from His own substance. Those men [may God keep from their opinion!] have still less sense than the others of whom we have spoken.

Our interpretation of this passage is confirmed in the same chapter, which notes that the belief to which it alludes is justified in the book of Job: "Whence then cometh wisdom, and where is the place of understanding? . . . God understandeth the way thereof, and He knoweth the place thereof" (Job 27:20, 23).

We find here, in fact, the names reserved by the *Zohar* for the three highest Sefiroth, which comprises all the others: viz., Wisdom, Intelligence and above them, Place or Non-Being (*non-être*)—so called because it represents the infinite, without attribute, without form, without any qualification—a state devoid of all reality, and therefore incomprehensible to us. It is in this sense, say the Kabbalists, that all that exists was drawn from Non-Being. The same author also gives us a psychological theory identical with that attributed to the school of Simeon ben Yohai, and he tells us that the dogma of pre-existence and transmigration of the soul, which is distinctly taught in the *Zohar*, was accepted in his time by several men who called themselves Jews and confirmed their extravagant opinion by the testimony of the Scriptures. Nor is this all. St. Jerome, in one of his letters, speaks of ten mystical names, *decem nomina mystica*, by which the Sacred Books designated the Divinity. Now, these ten names, which St. Jerome mentions and fully enumerates, are precisely the same that in the *Zohar* represent the ten Sefiroth or attributes of God.

This is what the "Book of Mystery" (*Sifra d'Zeniuta*), one of the most ancient fragments of the *Zohar*, in which are summarized the highest principles of the Kabbalah, says:

> When a man wishes to address a prayer to the Lord, he may invoke either the holy names of God: Eh-yeh, Jehovah, Yah, El, Elohim, Yedoud, Elohi-Zebaot, Shaddai, Adonai; or the ten Sefiroth, namely: the Crown, Wisdom, Intelligence, Beauty, Grace, Justice, etc.

All Kabbalists agree on the principle that the ten names of God and the ten Sefiroth are one and the same. For, they say, the spiritual part of the names of God is the very essence of the divine numbers. In several of his writings, St. Jerome also speaks of "certain Hebrew traditions on Genesis" which attribute to Paradise or, as it is always called in Hebrew, the Garden of Eden, a greater antiquity than to the world.

The only analogous Jewish traditions were those embodied in what the Talmud calls the Story of Genesis. Belief in those traditions is in perfect harmony with the *Zohar*, where the Supreme Wisdom, the Divine Word by which Creation was begun and accomplished, the principle of all intelligence and of all life, is designated as the True Eden, or the Higher Eden.

But most important of all is the intimate resemblance of the Kabbalah, in language and thought, to the gnostic sects, especially those which originated in Syria, and to the religious code of the Nazarene, discovered a few years ago and translated from the Syriac into Latin. Proof of this resemblance will be presented later in our study where the relationship between the kabbalistic system and other religious or philosophical systems is explored. At this point, note that the doctrines of Simeon the Magician, Elcsaite, Bardesanes and Valentine are known to us only through fragments scattered throughout the works of a few church fathers, such as Irenaeus and Clement of Alexandria. Now, we cannot suppose that those writings were familiar to a rabbi of the thirteenth century who, in the very work of which he is the presumed author, proves himself a stranger to any literature, and especially to that of Christianity. We are forced to admit that Gnosticism borrowed a great deal, if not precisely from the *Zohar* as we know it today, at least from its traditions and theories.

We shall not separate the hypothesis here refuted from the one which presents to us the Kabbalah as an imitation of the mystic philosophy of the Arabs, which came to the fore during the reign of the caliphs near the beginning of the eleventh century, when the philosophy of the Mussulmen first showed traces of mysticism. This opinion, long ago expressed as a mere conjecture, has recently been resuscitated by Tholuck, who has lent it the support of his rich erudition. In a preliminary memoir investigating the influence of Greek philosophy on that of the Muslims, the learned Orientalist concludes that the doctrine of emanation was known to the Arabs at the same time as Aristotle's system, which reached them through the commentaries of Themistius, Theon of Smyrna, Aeneus of Gaza and Johann Philoponus—that is to say, with the ideas of Alexandria albeit in a very incomplete form. This seed, once deposited in the soil of Islamism, developed rapidly into a vast system, which, like that of Plotinus, raised enthusiasm above reason. Claiming that all beings spring from divine substance, it proposed that man, as the last step toward perfection, reunite with that substance through ecstasy and annihilation of self.

It is this mysticism, half Arabic and half Greek, that Tholuck would have us accept as the true and only source of the Kabbalah. To that end he begins by attacking the authenticity of the kabbalistic books, particularly the *Zohar,* which he regards as a compilation dating from the end of the thirteenth century, although he accords greater antiquity to the Kabbalah itself. Tholuck then undertakes to demonstrate the close resemblance between the ideas contained in the Kabbalah and those which form the substance of Arabic mysticism. But since he advances no argument against the authenticity of the Kabbalah which we have not already refuted, we shall address ourselves only to the last and, undoubtedly, most interesting part of his work.

The first thought which comes to mind is that any similarity between the Hebrew and Arabic ideas, even if perfectly established, is no proof that the former were necessarily counterfeits of the latter. Is it not possible that both derived by different channels from one common source, much older than Muslim philosophy, much older even than the Greek philosophy of Alexandria? And Tholuck must concede that the Arabs knew the philosophy of Alexandria only at second hand. The works of Plotinus, Iamblicus and Proclus never reached them, and none of these authors had ever been translated either into Arabic or Syriac, while the works of Porphyrius contained only a purely logical commentary, the introduction to the treatise on the *Categories*.

On the other hand, is it probable that at the time of the Muslim invasion no trace was left of the ideas of ancient Persia and of the philosophy of the Magi, so famous throughout antiquity under the name of Oriental Wisdom, and that these ideas played no part in the intellectual movement which made the reign of the Abbassides so famous? We know that Avicenna wrote a book on Oriental Wisdom. By what right, then, can it be affirmed upon the strength of a few rare citations by a more modern author that the *Zohar* was but a collection of Neo-Platonic thoughts?

Tholuck directs our attention to a passage in Al Gazzali, Arab theologian and moralist (1580-1111): "Know that between the physical world and the one of which we just spoke, there exists the same relation as between our shadow and our body." How is it that he does not remember that the Zerdustians, members of one of the religious sects of ancient Persia, used the very same terms and the same comparison to formulate the fundamental principle of their belief?

As for the Jews, it is common knowledge that from the time of their captivity until their dispersion, they continued their relations with what they called the land of Babylon. We will not dwell upon this point, which is to be considered at length later. We will only note that the *Zohar* specifically quotes the Oriental Wisdom, "Known to the children of the East since the earliest days," as an example in perfect accord with its own doctrines. The citation does not refer to the Arabs, whom the Hebrew writers invariably call "the children of Ishmael" or "the children of Arabia." The *Zohar* could not have spoken of a contemporary foreign philosophy, a recent product of the influence of Aristotle and his Alexandrian commentators, in such terms—dating it from the first ages of the world; nor would it have presented this philosophy as a legacy transmitted by Abraham to the children of his concubine and, through them, to the nations of the Orient.

The truth is that Arab mysticism and the principles taught in the *Zohar* strike us by their differences rather than their similarities. Arab mysticism conveys a few general ideas common to all species of mysticism, while the *Zohar* illuminates the most essential points of the metaphysics of both systems, allowing no doubt regarding the diversity of their origins. Thus, to cite the most important of the differences: The Arab mystics, recognizing in God the unique substance of all things and the immanent cause of the universe, teach that He reveals or manifests Himself under three different aspects: that of unity or of absolute Being, where there is no differentiation as yet; that of differentiation, where the objects comprising the universe begin to separate into their essences and intelligible forms, presenting themselves to the Divine Intelligence; and that of the universe itself, the true world, God become visible.

The kabbalistic system is far more complicated. True, it also represents the divine substance as the unique substance, the inexhaustible source from which all life, all light and all existence flow eternally; but instead of three manifestations, three general forms of the Infinite Being, it recognizes ten—the ten Sefiroth, which subdivide into three trinities, and then unite in one single trinity and one supreme form. As a whole, the Sefiroth represent only the first degree, the first sphere, of existence—that which is called the World of Emanation. Below the Sefiroth, each separate and infinitely various, are the world of pure spirit or Creation; the world of spheres or of the intelligences directing them, called the World of Formation; and finally, the lowliest degree, called the World of Work or the World of Action.

The Arab mystics also recognize a collective soul, from which all the world-animating souls emanate, a generating spirit whom they call the father of spirits, the spirit of Mohammed, the source, model and substance of all other spirits.

An attempt has been made to find the model for Adam Kadmon, the Celestial Man of the Kabbalists, in this Arab concept. But what the Kabbalists mean by Adam Kadmon is not only the principle of intelligence and of spiritual life—something which they regard as both above and below the spirit—it is the totality of the Sefiroth, or the world of emanation in its entirety, from the Being in His most abstract and most intangible character, the "point" or Non-Being, to the constituent forces of nature. Not a trace of the idea of metempsychosis, which holds so important a place in the Hebraic system, can be found in the beliefs of the Arabs. And in vain do we search in their works for the allegories we meet in the *Zohar,* for that constant appeal to tradition, for those bold personifications which multiply by endless genealogies—*genealogis interminatis,* as St. Paul puts it in the first epistle to Timothy —for those gigantic and fantastic metaphors which are so compatible with the spirit of the ancient Orient.

At the end of his work, Tholuck himself, whose frankness matches his science, retracts his original thesis and concludes that it is impossible to consider the Kabbalah as derived from the mystic philosophy of the Arabs. In his own words, so authoritative because they come from a man profoundly learned in the philosophy and language of the Muslim people, he says:

> What can we conclude from the analogies? Very little, to my mind. For whatever is alike in the two systems will also be found in the more ancient doctrines, in the books of the Sabeans and the Persians, as well as among the Neo-Platonists. On the other hand, the extraordinary form in which those ideas appear in the Kabbalah is entirely strange to the Arab mystics. Besides, to be sure that the Kabbalah really derived from contact with Arab mystics, it would be necessary to find the Sefiroth in Arab mysticism. But not the least trace of the Sefiroth is to be found there; the Arab mystics recognized only one mode under which God revealed Himself. On this point, the Kabbalah comes much nearer to the doctrine of the Sabeans and to Gnosticism. . . .

Once the theory of the Arab origin of the Kabbalah has been proved inadmissible, the other theory, which makes the *Zohar* a work of the thirteenth century, loses its last support. The *Zohar* contains a highly important and widely embracing system. So large a conception is not formed in one day, especially in an age of ignorance and blind faith, and by a nation groaning under a heavy burden of contempt and persecution. And so, unable to find any of the antecedents or elements of the system of the Kabbalah in the Middle Ages, we must look for its origin in an earlier period.

What of the theory that Simeon ben Yohai really taught the metaphysical and religious doctrine (which forms the basis of the *Zohar*) to a small number of disciples and friends, among whom was his son; that these lessons, though transmitted at first by word of mouth as inviolable secrets, were gradually published; and that these traditions and notes, inescapably interwoven with more recent commentaries, accumulated and, by the same token, were altered with time, finally reaching Europe from Palestine towards the close of the thirteenth century? We hope that this opinion, until now hesitantly offered as conjecture, will soon acquire the character and rights of certainty.

For this theory is in perfect accord with the history of all the other religious monuments of the Jewish people. Like the Mishna and the Jerusalem and Babylonian Talmuds, the *Zohar* is a collection of the traditions of different ages and the lessons of different teachers, bound together by a common principle. This theory is in agreement with conviction which, as one historian notes, must be quite old: "I have learned from tradition that this work was so voluminous that when complete it would have made up a camel's load." Now, it cannot be supposed that even had he spent his whole life in writing on such matters, one man could have left such proof of his productiveness. Finally, in the Supplements to the *Zohar*, written in the same language and known for as long as the *Zohar* itself, it is stated that the latter will never be published in its entirety or, literally, that it will be disclosed only at the end of time.

Examining the book itself for some light on its origin, we soon perceive that it is utterly impossible to ascribe the *Zohar* to a single author. This is unmistakably conveyed by the unevenness of style (some passages are written almost entirely in Aramaic, while in other passages Aramaic terminations are appended to rabbinical Hebrew), and by the lack of unity, not in the system so much as in the exposition, method, application of general principles and consideration of details. Without multiplying important examples or insisting upon facts of language which no translation can preserve—just as it is impossible to tear certain plants from their native soil without killing them—we shall indicate the principal differences which distinguish the three fragments already mentioned from the rest of the work. The fragments are: the "Book of Concealment," generally considered the most ancient; the "Great Assembly," in which Simeon ben Yohai is shown amidst his friends, and finally the "Lesser Assembly," in which Simeon, on his deathbed, gives his last instructions to his surviving disciples.

Because of the long stretches between them, the fragments seem at first to be lost in the immense collection of kabbalistic writings. They form, however, a perfectly coordinated whole in the progress of events and ideas. In them are to be found, in allegorical or metaphysical language, a consecutive and circumstantial description of the divine attributes, their different manifestations, the manner in which the world was formed, and the relations between God and man. The author never descends from the heights of speculation to circumstantial and practical matters or to recommend observance of the Law or religious ceremonies. Nowhere do we find a name, a fact, or even a phrase to bring into question the authenticity of these pages, in which originality of form enhances lofty thoughts.

It is always the teacher speaking, using authority to convince his listeners. He does not demonstrate, or explain, or repeat what others have taught him. Instead, he affirms, and his every word is received as an article of faith. This characteristic is especially noticeable in the Book of Concealment, which is a substantial though very obscure summary of the entire work. The Latin aphorism is applicable: "He as though he had authority."

The *Zohar* gives the following graceful allegory about the "Book of Concealment":

> Let us picture to ourselves a man who lives alone in the mountains and knows nothing of the ways of the city. He sows wheat and eats nothing but wheat in its natural state. One day that man goes into the city. He is given a loaf of bread of good quality, and he asks: 'What is this good for?' They answer him: 'It is bread to eat.' He takes it and eats it with pleasure. Then he asks again: 'What is it made of?' They answer that it is made of wheat. Some time after that they give him a cake kneaded with oil. He takes it, then asks: 'And this, what is it made of?' They answer him—'Of wheat.' Somewhat later they set before him royal pastry kneaded with oil and honey. He asks the same question. Then he says: 'I am master of all these things. I taste them in the root, since I nourish myself from the wheat of which they are made.' With this thought he remains a stranger to the delights men find in eating, and those delights are lost to him. It is the same with the one who halts at the general principles of science; for he is ignorant of all the delights that are drawn from those principles.

The mode of procedure in the rest of the book is different. Rather than a continuous exposition of a given system of ideas in a freely conceived, consistently executed plan, in which the Second Texts are invoked to bear upon specific ideas instead of being introduced at random, the work is as incoherent and disordered as a commentary. Although, as already noted, the dissertation on the Holy Scriptures is only a pretext, this is not to say that without entirely abandoning the sphere of ideas itself, the text does not lead from one subject to another. This gives rise to the thought that the notes and traditions preserved in the school of Simeon ben Yohai were, in the spirit of the time, adapted to the principal passages of the Pentateuch instead of being welded into a conventional system based on logical order. This opinion is confirmed by the observation that there is often not the least connection between the biblical text and the part of the *Zohar* which serves it as a commentary.

The same incoherence and disorder reign among the facts, albeit these are few in number and much of a kind. Metaphysical theology is here no longer completely sovereign. Side by side with the boldest and most elevated theories are all too often to be found the most mundane details of external cult, or those puerile questions to which the Gemarists, like casuists of all other beliefs, devoted so many years and so many volumes. Everything—the form as well as the foundation—in this last portion of the book bears the traces of a more recent epoch; while the simplicity and naive credulous enthusiasm of the first portion often remind us of the time and language of the Bible.

We cite but one example from the last portion, the story of the death of Simeon ben Yohai, as told by Rabbi

Abba, the disciple to whom he entrusted the editing of his teachings.

> The Holy Light [so Simeon was called by his disciples] had as yet not finished the last phrase, when his words stopped; yet I continued to write. I had expected to write some time longer, when I heard nothing more. I did not lift my head, for the light was too strong to look at. Suddenly I was violently agitated, and I heard a voice crying: 'Long days, years of life and happiness are now before thee.' Then I heard another voice, which said: 'He asked Thee for life, and Thou hast given him eternal years.'
>
> All day the fire remained in the house, and no one dared come near him because of the fire and the light which surrounded him. All that day I lay stretched upon the ground and gave free rein to my lamentations. When the fire departed, I saw the Holy Light, the saint of saints, had departed from this world. He was stretched out, lying on his right side, with a smiling face. His son, Eleazar, arose, took his hands and covered them with kisses; but I would have gladly eaten the dust that his feet had touched.
>
> Then all his friends came to weep for him, but none could break the silence. At last their tears flowed. Rabbi Eleazar, his son, fell upon the ground three times, able to utter only the words: 'My father! My father!' Rabbi Hiah was first to rise. He said: 'Until today the Holy Light gave us light and watched over us; now we can do nothing but render him his last honors.' Rabbi Eleazar and Rabbi Abba arose to dress him in his cerements; then all his friends bewept him and all the house exhaled perfume. He was laid out on the bier by Rabbi Eleazar and Rabbi Abba alone. When the bier was carried away, they saw him on high and a brilliant light shone before

> his face. They they heard a voice that said: 'Come and assemble for the nuptial feast of Rabbi Simeon!'
>
> Such was Rabbi Simeon, son of Yohai, through whom the Lord glorified Himself each day. His part is beautiful in this world and in the world to come. Of him it was written: Go thy way toward the end, rest in peace and retain thy portion to the very end of time.

The passage contributes to an appreciation of the esteem in which Simeon was held by his disciples, and of the religious devotion his name inspired throughout the kabbalistic school.

There is another proof of the theory we espouse, which will undoubtedly be considered more conclusive. It is to be found in the following text, which we have nowhere seen cited, although it is included in every edition of the *Zohar*. After distinguishing between two kinds of masters, those of the Mishna and those of the Kabbalah, the text continues:

> It is of the latter that the prophet Daniel spoke when he said: 'And they that be wise shall shine as the brightness of the firmament.' He was referring to those who occupy themselves with the volume called the 'Book of Brightness' which, like Noah's Ark, takes in two from a city, and seven from a kingdom; but sometimes there is but one from a city, and two from a family. It is through them that the verse is fulfilled: 'Every male shall be cast into the river.' For the river is the light of this book.

These words are included in the *Zohar*, and yet it is evident that the *Zohar* was already in existence when they were written and was even known under the name it bears today. One is forced to conclude that it was formulated gradually, during the course of several centuries, and by the labors of several generations of Kabbalists.

Still another priceless passage demonstrates that long after the death of Simeon ben Yohai, his doctrine was preserved in Palestine, where he had lived and taught, and that emissaries were sent from Babylon to collect some of his words. Here, in substance, is what it says.

One day, when Rabbi Jose and Rabbi Hezekiah were traveling together, the conversation turned upon the verse of Ecclesiastes (3:19): "For that which befalleth the sons of men befalleth beasts; even one thing befalleth them; as the one dieth, so dieth the other; yea, they have all one kind of spirit." The two masters could not comprehend how King Solomon, the wisest of men, could have written the words which "open the door for those who have no faith." While reasoning thus, they were accosted by a man who, wearied by a long voyage in the hot sun, asked for water to drink. They gave him wine and led him to a spring. Upon being refreshed, the stranger told them that he was of their coreligionists and that through the mediation of his son, who devoted his entire time to the study of the Law, he had been initiated into this science. The question under discussion before his arrival was then submitted to him. It is not important to tell how the stranger resolved the question. It need only be said that he was roundly applauded and that it was with great reluctance that he was permitted to depart. Sometime later the two Kabbalists learned that this man was one of the Friends (this is what the adepts of the doctrine are called in the *Zohar*), who had been sent to Palestine by the Babylonian Friends to collect some of the sayings of Simeon ben Yohai and his disciples. One of the most renowned of the doctors of his time, it was out of humility that he had credited his son with the respect due himself.

All other facts recorded in this book are of the same hue and take place on the same stage. That there are frequent references to such Oriental religious beliefs as Sabeism and even Islamism while, on the contrary, there is none whatsoever to the Christian religion, proves that the *Zohar*, as presently constituted, could not have been introduced into Europe until some time near the end of the thirteenth century. Some of its doctrines, as Saadia has shown, were already known before then; but it seems certain that before Moses de Leon, and before the departure of Nahmanides for the Holy Land, there existed no complete manuscript in Europe.

As for the ideas contained in the *Zohar*, Simeon ben Yohai himself tells us that he was not the first to introduce them. He merely repeated to his disciples what the Friends taught in the ancient books. He mentions in particular, Jeba the Elder and Hamuna the Elder. He hopes that at the moment of revelation of the greatest secrets of the Kabbalah, the shade of Hamuna, followed by a procession of seventy of the Just, will come to listen. We do not pretend that either the persons or the books existed but only wish to establish that the authors of the *Zohar* never thought of representing Simeon ben Yohai as the inventor of the kabbalistic science.

There is another fact which deserves most serious attention. More than a century after the *Zohar* was published in Spain, there were still some men who knew and transmitted orally most of the ideas which constitute its substance. One such was Moses Botril who, in 1409, as he himself tells us, expressed himself on the Kabbalah and on the precautions to be taken in teaching it:

> The Kabbalah is simply a purer and holier philosophy,

> except that the language of philosophy is not the same as that of Kabbalah. . . . It is so named because it proceeds, not by argument, but by tradition. After the master has developed these matters for his disciple, the disciple must not have too much confidence in his own wisdom; he is not permitted to speak of this science until so authorized by the master. This right—that is to say, the right to speak about the Merkaba—will be accorded to him when he has given proof of his intelligence, and the seed deposited in his breast has borne fruit. On the other hand, it will be necessary to recommend silence to him if he is found to be superficial and if he has not as yet achieved the status of those who distinguish themselves by their meditations.

Botril seems not to have known the *Zohar* even by name, as it is nowhere mentioned in any part of his work. At the same time he cites a great many very ancient writers, nearly all from the Orient, such as Rabbi Saadia, Rabbi Hai, and Rabbi Aaron, head of the Babylonian Academy. Sometimes he writes of the oral teachings he has heard from his master, so it cannot be supposed that he drew his kabbalistic knowledge from the manuscripts published by Nahmanides and Moses de Leon. Still, the kabbalistic system, of which Simeon ben Yohai may be considered the most illustrious representative, was preserved and propagated after as well as before the thirteenth century, by a large number of traditions which some disciples put into writing, while others, more faithful to the method of their ancestors, guarded them religiously in their memory.

Only those traditions born between the first century and the latter part of the seventh century of the Christian era, are found in the *Zohar*. In fact, we cannot date them from an age less remote, as the Merkaba, which is merely the part of the Kabbalah to which the *Zohar* is dedicated, was already known then, and Simeon ben Yohai himself tells us that he had predecessors. It is equally impossible to date it later, for we know of no fact which authorizes such a conclusion.

Two more objections remain to be refuted. It has been asked how the principle underlying our present-day cosmography—the Copernican system—so clearly summed up in the passage translated above (*see* p. 41) could have been known before the seventh century, our outside date for the origin of the principal element of the kabbalistic system. The answer is that, even assuming the *Zohar* to be a thirteenth-century forgery, this passage antedates the birth of the Polish astronomer. The ideas contained in it were widespread among the ancients, as evidenced by the fact that Aristotle attributes them to the school of Pythagoras:

> Nearly all who claim to have studied the sky in its entirety mention that the earth is at the center; but the philosophers of the Italian school, otherwise known as the Pythagoreans, teach the contrary. In their opinion, the center is occupied by fire, and the earth is only a star whose circular movement around that center produces night and day.

The fathers of the church did not spare this opinion, which is in fact irreconcilable with the cosmological system taught in Genesis, from their attack against philosophy.

> It is [said Lactantius] an absurdity to believe that there are men whose feet are above their heads, and that there

> are countries where everything is upside down, where the trees and the plants grow upside down. . . . We find the seed of this error among the philosophers who claimed that the earth is round.

St. Augustine expresses himself on the same subject in very similar terms.

Finally, even the most ancient authors of the Gemara knew about the antipodes and spherical form of the earth. We read in the Jerusalem Talmud that this is why Alexander is represented with a globe in his hand. But the argument from Copernicus boomerangs, for throughout the Middle Ages the true structure of the universe was barely known, and the Ptolemaic theory held sway.

Here we close our purely bibliographic observations on the external history of the Kabbalah. The books we have examined are not, as enthusiasts have confidently affirmed, either of supernatural origin or of prehistoric antiquity. Neither are they, as a skeptical critic assumes, the product of an impostor motivated by sordid interest, devoid of ideas and convictions, and speculating in gross credulity. To repeat: These two books, the *Sefer Yetzirah* and the *Zohar*, are the product of several generations. Whatever may be the value of the doctrines they contain, they will always be worthy of preservation as a monument to the long patient struggle of a people for intellectual liberty at a time when religious despotism held sway. But this is not all. The system they encompass is, in itself, by reason of its origin and the influence it has exercised, a very important factor in the history of human thought.

Part Two

Analysis of the Doctrine

CHAPTER FOUR

The Sefer Yetzirah

DESPITE the credulity of some scholars and the skepticism of others, the two books which we have recognized as the true monuments of the Kabbalah furnish the material necessary for the explanation of this doctrine. Only on rare occasions, when the obscurity of the text makes it mandatory, will we make use of commentaries. But the innumerable fragments of which these books are composed, unselectively and uncritically borrowed from different epochs, are far from uniform in character.

Some fragments only extend the mythological system, whose most essential elements had already appeared in the Book of Job and the visions of Isaiah. Employing a wealth of detail they acquaint us with the functions of angels as well as of demons, making reference to ideas that were popular for too long a time to have been associated with a science considered since its origin to be as terrible as it was inviolable. Other fragments, undoubtedly the most recent, show so much bias and narrow-minded pharisaism as to resemble the talmudic traditions, mingling pride and ignorance with the views of a famous sect whose very name inspired idolatrous respect. Finally, the largest number of fragments, taken together, teach the true belief of the ancient Kabbalists. They attracted all those who, more or less interested in the philosophy of their time, wished to pass as the disciples and propagators of the ancient Kabbalists.

We must emphasize that the foregoing description applies only to the *Zohar*. The Book of Formation, which we shall analyze first, is not very extensive, nor does it always lift our minds to lofty regions. Nevertheless, it is a very homogeneous composition of rare originality. Instead of searching it for the mysteries of an ineffable science, we see it as an effort of awakening reason to perceive the plan of the universe and the bonds which unite all the various elements in one common principle.

Neither the Bible nor any other religious treatise has ever explained the world and the phenomena for which it is the stage except by leaning on the idea of God and setting itself up as the interpreter of the supreme will and thought. Thus, in the Book of Genesis light springs from nothingness, at the word of Jehovah. Having created the heavens and the earth from chaos, Jehovah judges His work and finds it worthy of His wisdom. To give light to the earth, He fastens the sun, the moon and the stars to the firmament. By taking dust and breathing life into it to create the last and most beautiful of His creatures, He declares His purpose to form man in His image.

In the work under discussion, the process is reversed —a very significant reversal when it occurs for the first time in the intellectual history of a people. It is the spectacle of the world that elevates mankind to the idea of God; it is the unity governing the work of Creation which demonstrates at one and the same time the oneness and wisdom of the Creator. That is why, as we have said before, the entire book is, as it were, a monologue by the patriarch Abraham; it is assumed that the reflections contained in the book are what led the father of the Hebrews from worship of the stars to worship of the Eternal God. This was remarked upon by the twelfth-century Spanish philosopher and Hebrew poet, Judah Halevi. "*Sefer Yetzirah* teaches the oneness and omnipotence of God by means of various examples, which are multiform on one side and uniform on the other. They are in harmony with regard to the One, their Director."

So far everything is within the bounds of reason. But instead of searching the universe for the laws that govern it thereby to learn about divine thought and wisdom, *Sefer Yetzirah* strives to draw a gross analogy between things and signs of thought, or the means by which wisdom makes itself heard to, and is preserved by, man. Note that mysticism always attaches immeasurable importance to outward representations of acts of intelligence. A well-known French writer once tried to prove that the art of writing was not a human invention, but a gift to humanity through revelation.

The twenty-two letters of the Hebrew alphabet and the first ten numbers, while preserving their own value, express the value of all other numbers. Taken collectively, these two types of symbols are called the thirty-two "marvelous paths of Wisdom" with which, says the text, "the Eternal, the Lord of Hosts, the God of Israel, the Living God, the King of the Universe, the God full of Mercy and Grace, the God sublime, Who dwells in Eternity, Whose name is high and holy, established His Name."

To these thirty-two paths of Wisdom we must add three other forms designated by three terms of very doubtful meaning, closely resembling the Greek terms for "subject," "object" and the "act of thought itself." As noted previously, these words are foreign to the text. Nevertheless, we must point out they were understood quite differently, in a way repugnant neither to the general character of the book nor to the laws of etymology, by Judah Halevi, who expressed himself as follows:

> As to *s'far*, it means the calculation and weighing of the created bodies. The calculation which is required for the harmonious and advantageous arrangement of a body is based on a numerical figure; expansion, measure, weight, relation of movements, and musical harmony—all these are based on the number expressed by the word *s'far*. No building emerges from the hand of the architect unless its image has first existed in his soul. *Sippur* signifies the language, or rather, the divine language, the voice of the words of the Living God. This produced the existence of the form which this language assumed in the words: 'Let there be light,' 'let there be a firmament.' The word was hardly spoken when the thing came into existence. This is also *sefer*, by which writing is meant. The writing of God means His creatures, the speech of God is His writing, the will of God is His speech. In the nature of God, therefore, *s'far, sippur* and *sefer*, are a unity, whilst they are three in human reckoning.

This interpretation has the merit of aptly describing this strange system that confounds the idea with the generally known symbols in order to make the ideal visible in the whole, as well as in the different parts of the universe.

Sefiroth is the term—it appears here for the first time—for the ten numbers or the abstract enumerations. They are represented as the most general and therefore the most essential forms of all that is—that is to say, as the categories of the universe. Thus, we must always meet with the number ten when searching for the prime elements or invariable principles of the world.

> There are ten Sefiroth; ten and not nine; ten and not eleven. Try to understand them in thy wisdom and thy intelligence; constantly train on them thy researches, thy speculations, thy knowledge, thy thought and imagination; rest all things on their principle, and restore the Creator on His foundation.

In other words, divine action as well as the existence of the world in the eyes of the intelligence take this abstract form of ten numbers, and each of the ten represents some infinity, either of space, time or some other attribute.

This, at least, is the meaning we attach to the following proposition: "There is no end to the ten Sefiroth, either in the future or in the past, either in good or in evil, either in height or in depth, either in the East or in the West, either in the South or in the North." Note that the different aspects under which the infinite is considered here, are ten—no more, no less. From this passage, we learn not only the general character of all the Sefiroth but to what elements and principles they correspond. Since the paired Sefiroth, although opposite, are part of one idea—one infinite—the text adds: "The ten Sefiroth are like the ten fingers, five pairs, but linked together by unity." The last words provide the explanation as well as the proof of all the preceding.

Without exactly deviating from the relations presented by outer things, this conception of the Sefiroth has an eminently abstract and metaphysical character. Were we to subject it to a strict analysis, we would find subordinated to the infinite and to absolute unity, the ideas of time, space, and of a certain unchangeable order without which there is neither good nor evil even in the sphere of the senses. But here is a somewhat different enumeration which, in appearance at least, assigns a greater importance to material elements.

> The first of the Sefiroth, One, is the spirit of the living God, blessed be His name, blessed be the name of the One Who lives in Eternity! The Spirit, the Voice, and the Word, that is the Holy Ghost.
>
> Two is the breath which issues from Spirit, it contains the twenty-two letters which form but one single breath.
>
> Three is water, which issues from breath or from air. In the water He dug darkness and void, mud and clay, and graved them in the shape of a garden bed.
>
> Four is fire, which issues from water, and with which He made the throne of His glory, the celestial wheels (*Ophanim*), the Seraphim and the angelic servitors. With the three together He built His habitation, and it was written: 'Who makest winds thy messengers, and the flaming fire, thy ministers.'

The next six numbers represent the different extremities of the world, that is to say, the four cardinal points (East, West, North and South), as well as height and depth.

Their symbols are the different combinations which may be formed with the first three Hebrew letters of the name Jehovah.

Thus, apart from the points in space, which in themselves hold nothing real, all the elements of which the world is composed evolved from one another, becoming more and more material the further they receded from their common origin, the Holy Spirit. Is not this what is called the doctrine of emanation? Is not this the doctrine which denies the popular belief that the world was evolved from nothing? The following words free us from uncertainty: "The end of the ten Sefiroth is tied to their beginning as the flame to the fire-brand, for the Lord is One and there is no second to Him: and what will you count before the One?"

To impress upon us that we are dealing with a great mystery, the next words are: "Chose your mouth that you speak not, and your heart that you do not ponder; and if your heart be too busy, bring it back to its place, for therefore it is said: run and return, and it is on this verse that a covenant was made." The last words probably alluded to some oath used by the Kabbalists to conceal their principles from the masses. The singular comparison contained in the first of the two passages is frequently repeated in the *Zohar;* we shall find it there enlarged, developed and applied to the soul as well as to God. Let us note that at all times and in all spheres of existence, in the consciousness as well as in external nature, creation through emanation has been represented by the radiation of flames or of light.

Another theory, famous in world thought, turns up here in a remarkable guise to merge with the theory of Sefiroth—the distinction between the two theories being more apparent than real. The second theory is that of the Word, or the Word of God, identified with His spirit and considered not only as the absolute form, but as the generating element and the very substance of the universe. Indeed, it is no longer a question, as in Onkelos' Chaldaic translation, of avoiding anthropomorphism by substituting divine thought and inspiration for God Himself wherever He intervenes as a human being in the biblical stories. *Sefer Yetzirah* expressly states, concisely and clearly, that the Holy or Divine Spirit and the Voice and the Word are one and the same thing, which has successively divested itself of all the elements of physical nature. Finally, it is not only what is called in the language of Aristotle "the material principle of things," but it is the Word become World. Moreover, we must bear in mind that this part of the Kabbalah deals only with the universe and not with man or humanity.

These reflections on the first ten numbers occupy a very distinct place in the Book of Formation. They apply to the universe in general and are more concerned with substance than with form. In the reflections we will now consider, the different parts of the universe are compared, and the same effort is made to bring them under a common law as was previously made to resolve them into a common principle, but more attention is paid to form than to substance. They have as their base the twenty-two letters of the Hebrew alphabet. But we must not forget the extraordinary role attributed to these symbols of thought in the first part of the work. Considered only in relation to the sounds they represent, the twenty-two letters stand, so to speak, on the boundary line between the intellectual and the physical world; though they can be resolved into one single material element, breath or air, they are characters indispensable to all languages and, consequently, the only possible or invariable aspect of the mind.

Neither the system as a whole nor its literal meaning permits a different interpretation of the words quoted above. "Two [the second principle of the universe] is the atmosphere which derives from the spirit; it is the breath in which are impressed the twenty-two letters which, all together, form but a single breath." Thus the simplest articulations of the human voice, the characters of the alphabet, play a role here quite similar to that played by ideas in Plato's philosophy. It is by their presence, by the impression they leave on things, that we recognize a Supreme Intelligence throughout the universe; and it is, finally, through them that the Holy Spirit reveals Itself in nature. That is the meaning of the following proposition: "By giving the twenty-two letters form and figure, and by mixing and combining them in different ways, God made the soul of all that is formed and of all that shall be formed. And on these same letters the Holy One, blessed be He, founded His sublime and holy name."

The letters are divided into different classes, called "three mothers," "seven doubles," and "twelve simples." The function of the letters is wholly supplanted by the numerical division that has been noted; or, more explicitly, an attempt, right or wrong, is made to find the numbers three, seven and twelve in the three areas of nature:

1. In the general composition of the world;
2. In the division of the year or in the distribution of time of which the year is the principal unit; and
3. In the structure of man.

Although not stated explicitly, we find here the idea of the macrocosm and the microcosm, or the belief that man is only an image or, so to speak, the epitome of the universe.

In the general composition of the world, mothers—that is to say, the number three—represent the elements: water, air and fire. Fire is the substance of the heavens; by condensation water becomes the substance of the earth; air lies between these two antagonistic principles, which it separates and reconciles by domination. Three also brings to mind the principal seasons of the year: summer, which corresponds to fire; winter, which in the East is generally marked by rains or by the predominance of water; and the temperate season, which results from the union of spring and autumn. The same trinity, finally, is seen in the structure of the human body: the head, the heart and the stomach. These are, if I am not mistaken, the functions of the different organs which a modern physician has called "'the tripod of life."

The number three seems here, as in all other mystical combinations, to be so indispensable a form that it is the symbol of the moral man in whom is discernible "the scale of merit, the scale of culpability, and the language of the law which decides between the two."

The seven doubles represent the contraries, or such things as may serve two opposite ends. There are seven planets in the universe, whose influence is now good, now bad; there are seven days and seven nights in the week; there are seven doorways to the human body: the eyes, the ears, the nostrils and the mouth; and, finally, the number seven is also the number of happy or unhappy events which may occur to a human being. But this classification is too arbitrary to deserve a place in this analysis.

The twelve simples correspond to the twelve signs of the zodiac, to the twelve months of the year, to the principal parts of the human body, and to the most important attributes of our nature: sight, hearing, smell, speech, nutrition, generation, action or touch, locomotion, anger, laughter, thought and sleep. This is the beginning of the spirit of investigation; surprising though its methods may be, that itself is proof of its originality.

Thus, the material form of intelligence, represented by the twenty-two letters of the alphabet, is also the form of all that is; for, beyond man, the universe and time, nothing but the infinite can be conceived. These three concepts are also called "the faithful witnesses of truth." Despite their variations, each constitutes a system with its own center and hierarchy. "For," says the text, "the one prevails over the three, the three over the seven, and the seven over the twelve, but each part of the system is inseparable from the other parts." The Celestial Dragon is the center of the universe, the heart is the center of man, and, finally, the revolutions of the zodiac constitute the basis of the years. The first, it is said, is comparable to a king upon his throne; the second to a king among his subjects; the third to a king in war.

We believe that this comparison points to the perfect order reigning in the universe, and the contradictions which exist in man without destroying his unity. In fact, it is added, the twelve principal organs of man's body

> are aligned one against another, as in order to battle. Three of them serve love, three produce hatred, three give life and three cause death. Thus evil confronts good, and from evil comes forth evil alone, just as good gives birth only to good.

But immediately the remark is made that none can be understood without the others.

Finally, above these three systems, above man, above the universe, and above time; above the letters of the alphabet as well as the numbers of the Sefiroth "is the Lord, the True King Who reigns over all things from the place of His holiness forever and ever." Following these words, which form the true conclusion of the book, comes the dramatic climax—the conversion of Abraham, the idol worshipper, to the religion of the True God.

The system culminates with the substitution of absolute unity for every form of dualism—the dualism of pagan philosophy, which would find in matter an eternal substance whose laws are not always in accord with the Divine Will, as well as the dualism of the Bible. Although the biblical concept of Creation views the Divine Will, and consequently the Infinite Being, as the only cause, the only real source of the world, at the same time it regards these two, the universe and God, as two absolutely distinct and separate substances. In the *Sefer Yetzirah,* God is really considered as the Infinite Being and therefore indefinable; God, in the fullness of His power and existence, is above, but not outside, the letters and numbers—that is to say, not outside the principles and laws which we distinguish in this world.

Each element has its source in a superior element, and all elements have their common origin in the Word or in the Holy Spirit. It is in the Word also that we find those invariable signs of thought, which repeat themselves in one form or another in all the spheres of existence, and through which all that exists (or *is*) becomes an expression of the same design. And that Word itself, the first number, the most sublime of all the things we can count and define—what is it but the most sublime and most absolute of the manifestations of God—that is, supreme thought or intelligence? Thus, in the highest sense, God is both the matter and the form of the universe. And not only is He *this* matter and *this* form, but nothing exists or can exist outside Him. His substance is at the bottom of everything, and therefore all things bear His imprint and are symbols of His supreme intelligence.

This bold deduction is the basis of the doctrine set forth in the *Zohar*. But the exposition is entirely different from the one we have outlined. Instead of gradually, by an inductive comparison of the particular forms and subordinate principles of this world, leading up to the supreme principle, the universal form, and, finally absolute unity, it is the conclusion, the absolute unity, that is first asserted. It is assumed and invoked on every occasion as an undisputed axiom. True, the connection between all the deductions is broken by the exterior shape of the work, but the synthetic character which permeates it is pronounced and visible.

We may say, then, that the Book of Brightness (or the Book of Splendor) begins at the very point where the Book of Formation ends. The conclusion of the one serves as the premise of the other. A second, more important, difference finds its explanation in a general law of the human mind. We see inner forms, invariable concepts—in a word, *ideas,* in the broadest and noblest sense of the word—substituted for letters and numbers. The divine word, Logos, instead of manifesting itself exclusively in nature, appears primarily in man and in intelligence; it is called the Archetype or Celestial Man: Adam Kadmon.

In certain fragments, whose great antiquity cannot be contested, we see thought itself taken for universal substance, without prejudice to absolute unity, and the regular development of this power substituted for the somewhat gross theory of emanation. Far be it from us to pretend to discover among the ancient Hebrews the philosophical doctrine which practically dominates Germany today [1843—ed.]; but we maintain, and hope to demonstrate, that the principle of that doctrine, and even the expressions appropriated by the school of Hegel, are to be found in the forgotten traditions we are now endeavoring to bring to light.

This transformation of symbol into idea in the Kabbalah is reproduced in all great philosophical and religious systems and in all great conceptions of the human intellect. Do we not see the linguistic forms of Aristotle's logic, which underlies rationalism, evolve in Kant's logic into categories? In idealism, did not Pythagoras and the system of numbers precede the sublime theory of Plato? And in social thought, were not all men represented as issuing from the same blood? Was not their fraternity found in the flesh before it was found in the identity of their duties and their rights, or in the uniformity of their natures and functions? This is not the place for further insistence upon a general matter of fact, but we hope to have clarified the relations existing between the *Sefer Yetzirah* and the more extensive and important *Zohar*.

CHAPTER FIVE

The Zohar: Allegorical Method of the Kabbalists

THE CONTRIBUTORS to the *Zohar* presented their ideas in the most obscure and least logical way—as a simple commentary on the Five Books of Moses. It is important, then, to know how they understood the interpretation of the sacred Scriptures, and how they succeeded in using biblical commentary as a support at the very moment that they deviated most from the plain sense of the Bible. For this is their method of interpretation and, generally speaking, symbolic mysticism has no other basis. In the Kabbalists' own words:

> Woe to the man who sees nothing but simple stories and ordinary words in the Law! For were this so, we could even nowadays frame a law which would deserve higher praise. Were it our desire to find nothing but simple words, all we should need do is turn to the legislators of the earth, many of whom possess greatness. It would be sufficient to initiate them and to make a law according to their words and their example. But it is not so; every word of the Law holds an exalted meaning and a sublime mystery.
>
> The recitals of the Law are the vestment of the Law. Woe to him who takes that vestment for the Law itself! David had this in mind when he said: 'Open Thou, my eyes, that I may behold wondrous things out of Thy law' [i.e., what is hidden under the cloak of the Law—Ps. 119:18].
>
> There are foolish people who, when they see a man dressed in fine clothing, look no further than the garment, and yet it is the body that lends value to the clothes; still more precious is the soul. The Law also has its body. There are commandments that may be called the body of the Law, and the ordinary recitals which are mingled with them are the clothes which cover the body. The simple-minded heed only the vestments of the recitals of the Law; they know nothing else and do not see what is hidden under this garment. The well-informed think not of the vestment, but of the body that the vestment covers. Finally, the wise, servants of the Supreme King, they who dwell upon the heights of Sinai, think only of the soul, which is the foundation of all the rest, and is the Law itself, and in time to come they will be prepared to contemplate the spirit of that spirit which breathes in the Law.

Thus, by the ingenuous or disingenuous assumption of

a mysterious meaning unknown to the profane, the Kabbalists first placed themselves above the historic facts and positive precepts which constitute the Scriptures. This was their only means of assuring themselves full liberty without openly breaking with religious authority; possibly, they also felt the need of assuaging their consciences. We find the same spirit in a still more remarkable form:

> If the Law consisted of nothing but ordinary words and recitals, like the words of Esau, Hagar, Laban, Balaam's ass and Balaam himself, why should it have been called the Law of truth, the perfect Law, the faithful testimony of God? Why should the wise man deem it more precious than gold and pearls? But it is not so. Every word conceals a most elevated meaning; every recital contains more than the events it seems to contain. And this higher and more holy Law is the true Law.

It is of some interest to find similar views and expressions in the works of a church father:

> Were we obliged [says Origen] to hold to the letter of the Law and to understand what is written in the laws as the Jews and the people understand it, I should blush to proclaim that it is God who gave us such laws; I should find more grandeur, and more reason in the laws of man as, for instance, in the laws of Athens, Rome or Lacedemonia. . . .
>
> What sensible man, pray, could be made to believe that the first, second and third days of the Creation, where morning and evening are mentioned, could exist without sun, moon and stars; that on the first day there was not even a sky; where will we find a mind so limited as to believe that God devoted Himself like a farmer to the planting of trees in the Garden of Eden, situated to the

> East; that one of the trees was the tree of life, and that another could give knowledge of good and evil? I think that no one will hesitate to regard these as façades behind which mysteries are hidden.

Finally, Origen differentiates between a historical meaning, a moral, and a mystical one; but instead of using clothes as a simile, he likens the historical meaning to the body, the moral to the soul, and the mystic to the spirit. To establish certain apparent relations between the sacred word and these arbitrary interpretations, the ancient Kabbalists sometimes resorted to arbitrary systems very rarely encountered in the *Zohar* but accorded considerable space by modern Kabbalists. There are three such systems: One, Gematria, consists in setting one word in place of another which has the same numerical value; the second, Notarikon, makes each letter of one word the initial of another word; in the third, Tomurah, the value of the letters is changed: for instance, the last letters take the place of the first, and vice versa. Since these systems never serve as the basis of any important idea and have been much discussed, we move on to the essential subject of our researches—the doctrine which serves as the unifying basis of what purports to be commentaries on the Scriptures.

We shall first seek to present the nature and attributes of God, in the light of the most ancient fragments of the *Zohar*. Then we shall set forth the idea these fragments give us of the formation of beings in general, or of the relations of God with the universe. Finally, we shall consider man—what the *Zohar* conceives to be his chief aspects, and its description of his origin, nature and destiny.

CHAPTER SIX

The Zohar: The Kabbalist Conception of the Nature of God

THE KABBALISTS speak of God in two different ways, a fact which in no way impairs the unity of their thought. When they seek to define God, to draw attention to His attributes and give us a precise idea of His nature, they speak in the language of metaphysics, with all the lucidity demanded by this subject and in its idiom. But at other times they represent the divinity as a Being Which cannot be comprehended at all, Which dwells forever outside of any shape with which we may, in imagination, invest it. At such times their expressions are poetical and figurative, and they combat imagination with its own weapons; then all their efforts tend to destroy anthropomorphism by assigning it such gigantic proportions that the frightened mind, unable to find any term of comparison, is compelled to trust in the idea of the Infinite.

The Book of Concealment is written entirely in this style; but as the allegories it employs are all too often puzzling, a passage of the *Idra Rabba* may confirm our point. (These two words, *Idra Rabba,* signify the Great Assembly; the fragment bearing this title comprises the discourses Simeon ben Yohai delivered to all his ten disciples. At a later time when death had reduced them to the number of seven, they formed the Little Assembly, which ben Yohai addressed on his deathbed.)

> Simeon ben Yohai had just assembled his disciples. He told them that the time had come to work for the Lord—that is to say, to make known the real meaning of the Law; that his days were numbered, that the laborers were few, and the voice of the Lord was being more and more urgent. He made them swear that they would not profane the mysteries he was about to confide to them. They repaired to a field and sat down in the shadows of the trees. Simeon was about to break the silence when a voice was heard and their knees knocked against one another with fear. What was that voice? It was the voice of the celestial assembly which had gathered to listen. Rabbi Simeon exclaimed joyfully: Lord, I have heard Thy voice [Habakkuk 3:1], but I shall not add as that prophet did, 'I am afraid,' for this is not the time to fear; it is the time to love, as it is written: Thou shalt love the Lord, thy God.

This solemn introduction is followed by a long, entirely allegorical, description of the divine greatness. We paraphrase:

> He is the Ancient of the Ancients, the Mystery of Mysteries, the Unknown of Unknowns. He has a form peculiar to Himself, appearing to us as the preeminently Aged, as the Ancient of Ancients, as the Unknown among the Unknowns. But in the form that we know Him, He still remainst unknown to us. His vestment seems white, and His appearance is brilliant.
>
> He is seated on a throne of fiery sparks which He subjects to His will. The white light emitted by His head illumines four hundred thousand worlds. This white light becomes the inheritance of the just in the world to come. Each day sees thirteen myriads of worlds kindled by His brain; He sustains them, and He alone bears their weight. From his head He sprinkles a dew which rouses the dead to a new life. For that is the meaning of the writ [Isa. 26:19]: For Thy dew is as the dew of light. It is this dew which is the nourishment of the greatest saints. It is the manna prepared for the just in the life to come. It falls in the fields of the 'sacred fruits.' The aspect of that dew is white as the diamond whose color contains all colors. . . . The length of that face, from the summit of the skull, is three hundred and seventy thousand myriad worlds, and it is called the long face, for such is the name of the Ancient of the Ancients.

In this final passage, the long or great face is the divine substance, the first of the Sefiroth, as we shall soon see.

However, we should fail the truth were we to give the impression that the rest of the *Zohar* can be judged by this example. The oddness, affection and convention, with which Orientals so often abuse allegory, are more evident here than nobility and grandeur. The head, dazzling with light, which represents the eternal hearth of life and learning, becomes a kind of subject for anatomical study; neither the forehead, face, eyes, brain, hair, nor beard—

nothing is overlooked; everything offers an opportunity to enunciate numbers and propositions describing the Infinite. This, evidently, is what provoked the charges of anthropomorphism, and even materialism, which some modern writers have directed against the Kabbalists. But neither the accusation nor the style which evoked it are worthy of further consideration. Let us rather attempt to translate some of the fragments in which the same subject is so treated as to be of greater interest to philosophy and the history of human intelligence.

Our first fragment is very large. Under pretense of elucidating the true meaning of the words of Isaiah (40: 25), "To whom then will ye liken me, that I shall be equal? saith the Holy One," it explains the genesis of the ten Sefiroth or chief attributes of God, and the nature of God Himself, though He be concealed in His own substance.

> Before having created any form in the world, before having produced any image, He was alone, without form, without resemblance to anything. Who could conceive Him as He was then, before the Creation, since He was formless? It is therefore forbidden to represent Him by any image, by any form whatever, even by His holy name, even by a letter or by an iota. That is the meaning of the words (Deut. 4:15), 'For ye saw no manner of form on the day that the Lord spake unto you.' That is to say, you saw nothing that you can represent under any form or by any image. But after having produced the form of the Heavenly Man (Adam E-lo-oh), He used it as a chariot (Merkaba) to descend; He wished to be called by that form which is the holy name of Jehovah; He wished to be known by His attributes, by each attribute separately, and permitted Himself to be called the God of Mercy, the God of Justice, the All Powerful God,

the God of Hosts, and the One Who Is. His intention was to make known His qualities and how His justice and His mercy embrace the world as well as the work of man. Had He not shed His light over all creatures, how could we have known Him? How would it be true to say that 'the whole earth is full of His glory?' (Isa. 6:3.) Woe to the man who dares compare Him even to one of His own attributes! Even less may He be likened to man, born of earth and destined to death. He must be conceived as above all creatures and above all attributes.

There is neither attribute, nor image, nor figure when all these have been taken away; what remains may be compared to a sea, for the waters of the sea are in themselves limitless and without form; but when they spread over the earth they produce an image (*Dimyon*). We can make the following calculations: the source of the waters of the sea, and the jet springing from it to cover the ground, make two. Then an immense basin forms, as a basin is formed when a pit of vast depth is dug; that basin is filled by the waters which have sprung from the source—and that is the sea itself, which should be counted as number three. The vast depth divides into seven canals which resemble seven long vessels. The source, the jet, the sea and the seven canals, together, make ten. If the Master who constructed those vessels breaks them, the waters return to their source, and only the dry fragments of the vessels remain. Thus, the Cause of Causes produced the ten Sefiroth. The Crown is the source from which an unending light springs forth, hence the name Infinite (Ayn Sof) to designate the Supreme Cause, for in that state it has neither form nor countenance; therefore, there is no means of comprehending it and no way of knowing it; and that is the meaning of the verse, 'Meditate not upon that which is too far above thee and investigate not that which what is covered from thee.' Then a vessel comes into existence, as tiny as an iota—as the [Hebrew] letter Yod—which, nevertheless, the divine light penetrates. This is the source of Wisdom; it is Wisdom, by virtue of which the Supreme Cause takes the name of the All-Wise God. After which it constructs a great vessel like the sea, called the Intelligence, whence the name of God as the 'Intelligent.' However, let us remember that God is good and wise by virtue of Himself; for Wisdom does not deserve its name because of its own virtue, but because of Him Who is wise and Who produces Wisdom from the light emanated from Him. Neither is Intelligence conceivable of itself, but through Him Who is the Intelligent and Who replenishes it from His own substance. He need only withdraw for Intelligence to drain dry. That is the meaning of the verse (Job 14:11), 'And the waters fall from the sea and the river is drained dry.'

Finally, the sea is divided into seven branches: from these issue the seven precious vessels called Mercy or Grandeur, Justice or Strength, Beauty, Triumph, Glory, Kingdom and the Foundation or Basis. Hence, He is called the Great or the Merciful, the Strong, the Magnificent, the God of Victory, the Creator to whom all glory belongs, and the Foundation of all things. The last attribute sustains all the others, as well as all the worlds. Finally, He is the King of the Universe; for all things are in His power. He can diminish the number of vessels, and He can increase the light which breaks forth from them, or the contrary, if He prefers.

Almost the entire Kabbalist view of the nature of God is summed up in this text. But the text still leaves some confusion. On the one hand, it needs to be considerably developed; on the other hand, each of the principles requires a more exact and precise truth and without substituting our own ideas for those of the text, we shall reduce the passage to a few fundamental propositions, each one of which will be elucidated and at the same time justified by other extracts from the *Zohar*.

1. God is above all the Infinite Being; He cannot therefore be considered as the totality of beings or as the sum of His own attributes. But without these attributes and without the effects which result from them—that is to say, without a definite form—it is never possible either to comprehend or to know Him. This principle is clearly expressed: "Before the Creation God was without form, resembling nothing; and in this state no intelligence could conceive him." The same thought is to be recognized in the following passage:

> Before God manifested Himself, when all things were still hidden in Him, He was the least known of all the unknowns. In that state He had no name other than that which expresses interrogation. He began by forming an imperceptible point; that was His own thought. With this thought He then began to construct a mysterious and holy form; finally He covered it with a rich radiant garment—that is to say, the universe, whose name necessarily enters into the name of God.

Incidentally, this text contains a play upon words that cannot be rendered literally. It is based on an interpretation of the verse: "Lift up your eyes on high and see Who hath created these" (Isa. 40:26). Now, combining the two Hebrew words: *me* (who) and *eyleh* (these), one produces the name of God (*Elohim*). The *Zohar* concludes that the universe and God are inseparable, since both have one and the same name.

The *Idra Zuta* further states:

> The Ancient of Ancients is at the same time the Unknown of Unknowns; He separates Himself from all things yet He is not separated; for all things unite with Him, as He reunites with all; there is nothing that is not in Him. He has a form yet it may be said He has no form. But assuming a form He gave existence to all that is; first, He caused His form to send out nine lights, which shine by virtue of the form they borrowed of Him, diffusing a dazzling effulgence on all sides, as a beam disperses its luminous rays. The Ancient of Ancients, the Unknown of Unknowns, is a high beacon which is recognized only by the rays dazzling our eyes with their brilliant abundance. This light is called His holy name.

2. The ten Sefiroth by which the Infinite Being first manifested Himself are merely His attributes, which have no substantial reality of their own. In each of these attributes the divine substance is present in its entirety; taken all together, they constitute the first, most complete, and highest of all the divine manifestations. It is called the archetypal or celestial man (Adam Kadmon, Adam E-lo-oh). This is the figure which dominates Ezekiel's mysterious chariot and of which terrestrial man is but a faint copy.

> The form of man [says Simeon ben Yohai to his disciples] contains all that is in heaven above and upon earth below, the superior as well as the inferior beings; it is for that reason that the Ancient of Ancients has chosen it for His own. No form, no world could exist before the human form came into existence, for the human form contains all things, and all that is, exists only by virtue of it: without it there would be no world, for as the writ says (Prov. 3:19), 'The Lord by wisdom founded the earth.'

It is necessary to distinguish between higher man (Adam d'leeloh) and lower man (Adam d'letatoh), for one could not exist without the other. On the higher form of man rests the perfection of faith in all things, and it was of that form that the prophet Ezekiel spoke when he said that he saw above the chariot the likeness of a man; and it is of that form that Daniel said (Dan. 7:13), "I saw in the nightly visions, and behold, there came with the clouds of heaven, one like unto the son of man and he came even to the Ancient of days, and he was brought near before Him." Thus, what is called celestial man, or the first divine manifestation, is merely the absolute form of all that exists; the source of all the other forms, or rather of all ideas, the supreme thought, otherwise known as the *Logos* or the Word. This is not a simple conjecture but an historical fact, the accuracy of which will be more appreciated as our knowledge of the system is enlarged. We cite yet another passage: "The form of the Ancient (Whose name be sanctified!) is a unique form which embraces all forms. It is the supreme and mysterious Wisdom which contains all the rest."

3. The ten Sefiroth, if we may believe the authors of the *Zohar*, are indicated in the Old Testament by as many special names consecrated to God—the same ten mystical names quoted by St. Jerome in his letter to Marcella. An attempt is also made to find these names in the Mishna, which says that God created the world with ten words, or by as many orders issued through His sovereign word. Although all the names are equally necessary, the attributes and distinctions they express do not provide identically sublime conceptions of the divine nature; they represent it under different aspects, called in the language of the Kabbalists "faces."

Simeon ben Yohai and his disciples make frequent use of this metaphor, but they do not abuse it as have their modern successors. We shall dwell on this point because it is unquestionably the most important in the entire kabbalistic science. Before determining the particular character of each of the Sefiroth, we shall glance at the general question of their essence and set forth in a few words the different opinions to which they gave rise among the adepts of the doctrine of the Kabbalah.

All Kabbalists have raised two questions: First, *Why* are there Sefiroth? Then, *what* are the Sefiroth—in themselves, or in relation to God?

As to the first question, the texts of the *Zohar* leave not the slightest doubt. There are Sefiroth as there are names of God, the two being confused in the mind, and the Sefiroth being the ideas and things expressed by names. Now, if God could not be named, or if all His names did not designate a real thing, not only would we not know Him, but He would not exist even to Himself; for without Intelligence He could not comprehend Himself, nor could He be wise without Wisdom, or act without Power.

The second question, though, has not been answered by all scholars in the same manner. Some, beginning with the principle that God is immutable, regard the Sefiroth as instruments of the Divine Power, creatures of a superior nature, but entirely different from the First Being. They would reconcile the language of the Kabbalah with the letter of the Law. At the head of this group stands Menahem Recante, the author of the book, *The Motives of the Commandments,* who wrote at the beginning of the thirteenth century. Other scholars, carrying to its logical conclusion the old principle that nothing can come from nothing, identify the ten Sefiroth completely with the divine substance. That which the *Zohar* calls Ayn Sof, i.e., the Infinite Himself, is in their opinion the totality of the Sefiroth—no more, no less—each of the Sefiroth being but a different point of view of the same Infinite.

Between these two extremes stands a third viewpoint, much more profound and in accord with the spirit of the original kabbalistic writings. This viewpoint does not consider the Sefiroth to be instruments, creatures and, consequently, beings distinct from God, nor is it willing to identify them with God. Those who take this middle position assert: God is present in the Sefiroth, otherwise He could not reveal Himself through them; but He does not dwell in them in His entirety. He is more than that which is found in the sublime forms of thought and existence. In fact, the Sefiroth can never comprise the Ayn Sof, which is the very source of every form and which, in this capacity, has no form; or, to use ordinary terms, while each one of the Sefiroth has a name, the Infinite alone has not and cannot have one. God remains, therefore, the Ineffable Being—incomprehensible, infinite, high above all the worlds that reveal His presence, even the world of emanation.

This interpretation of the Sefiroth takes divine immutability into account. For the ten Sefiroth may be compared to ten different-shaped vases or different-colored glasses. Whichever vessel we measure, its absolute essence remains the same, and the divine light, like the light of the sun, is not altered in nature by the medium through which it passes. These vessels and these media have no reality in themselves; they have no existence of their own; they simply represent the limits within which the Supreme Essence of things has confined itself, the different degrees of obscurity with which the Divine Light veils its infinite brightness, so that it may be viewed. Hence the desire to recognize in the Sefiroth two elements, or rather, two different aspects: one, purely external and negative, representing the body, the so-called vessel; the other, internal, positive, representing the spirit and the light.

Thus the Kabbalists speak of broken vessels which let the divine light escape. This point of view is adopted by Isaac Luria, in his *Sefer Drushim,* a work translated into German by Knorr von Rosenroth and included in *The Kabbalah Unveiled.* It is also the view adopted by Moses Cordovera, who presents it with logic and precision in *Pardes Rimonim* (*The Garden of Pomegranates*). In addition to his lucidity, Cordovera deserves praise for reporting correctly and discussing profoundly the opinions of his predecessors and adversaries. His presentation is historically the most exact, and we shall rely on it as the basis for all interpretations of the metaphysical part of the Kabbalah.

What is the specific role of each of the Sefiroth? How are the Sefiroth grouped?

The first and highest of all the divine manifestations—in a word, the first of the Sefiroth—is the Crown (Kether), so named because it is above all the others: "the principle of all principles, the mysterious wisdom, the highest of all crowns with which all diadems and crowns are adorned." It is not the confused totality, without form or name, the mysterious unknown that preceded all things, even the attributes—the Ayn Sof. Rather, the Crown represents the Infinite as distinguished from the finite; its name in Holy Writ signifies "I am," because it is absolute being, being which analysis cannot plumb, which cannot be qualified, but in which all qualifications unite in one indivisible point. Hence, the first Sefiroth is also called the "primitive point" or simply the "point": "When the Unknown of Unknowns wished to manifest Himself, He first produced one point. So long as this luminous point was part of Him, the Infinite was as yet completely unknown and shed no light at all." This is what the later Kabbalists explained as the absolute concentration of God in His own substance (Tsimtsum). This concentration brought forth space, "primitive air"—not a true void, but a degree of light inferior to the Creation. But because God retired within Himeslf, He is distinct from all that is finite, limited and determined, and because what He is cannot yet be determined, He is designated by a word which signifies "no-thing," or non-being (Ayn).

"He is so named," says *Idra Zuta,* "because we do not know and cannot know what is in this [principle,] because it is unattainable within our limitations and is above wisdom itself." We find the same idea, even the same phrasing, in one of the greatest and most famous systems of modern metaphysics, that of Hegel:

> Everything begins *with a pure state of being,* a wholly indeterminate, simple and immediate thought, for the true beginning can be nothing else. . . . This pure being is only the purest abstraction; it is an absolute negative term which may be called the *non-existent* if conceived in an immediate manner.

Finally, to return to our Kabbalists, the very idea of being, or of the Absolute, constituted a complete form, or, to use their term, a head, a face. Sometimes they call it "white head" because in it are blended all colors, that is to say, all ideas, all definite aspects; sometimes they call it the "ancient" because it is the first of the Sefiroth;

this should not be confused with the "Ancient of Ancients," that is to say, with the Ayn Sof Himself, before Whom the most dazzling light is but a shadow. But it is usually designated with the singular name of "long face," undoubtedly because it contains all the other qualifications and all the intellectual and moral attributes from which the "small face" is formed. "The first," says the *Zohar* text, "is the Ancient, seen face to face. It is the supreme head, the source of all light, the principle of all wisdom, and can be defined only as unity."

From this absolute unity, distinct from the various forms and from all relative unity, issue two parallel principles, opposite in appearance but inseparable in reality. One, male or active, is called Wisdom; the other passive, or female, is designated by a word customarily translated as intelligence. "All that exists," says the text, "all that has been formed by the Ancient (Whose name be sanctified!) can exist only in a male and a female."

Wisdom is also called Father, for Wisdom engenders all things. Diffused through the universe, in thirty-two marvelous ways, it imposes a form and measure on all that is. Intelligence is Mother in keeping with the verse: "Thou shalt call understanding, mother." (Prov. 2:3). Without destroying the male-female antithesis established as the general condition of existence, the *Zohar* often has the female or passive principle spring forth from the male principle. From their mysterious and eternal union comes forth a son, who takes on the features of both father and mother, bearing witness to both of them. This son of Wisdom and Intelligence, also called First-born, is knowledge or Science.

These three persons contain and unite all that was, is, and will be; but they in turn are reunited in the white head, in the Ancient of Ancients, for *all* is He, and *He* is all and in all. At times he is represented with three heads which form but one head; at times he is compared to the brain which, without losing its unity, is divided into three parts, and by means of thirty-two pairs of nerves permeates the entire body, as Divinity permeates the universe through the thirty-two ways of Wisdom.

> The Ancient (Whose name be sanctified!) exists with three heads which form but one head, and that head is the most exalted among the most exalted things. And because this Ancient (Whose name be blessed!) is represented by the number three, all the other lights [the other Sefiroth] which receive light from Him, are also comprised in the number three.

In the following passage the terms of that trinity are somewhat different. We see the Ayn Sof Himself, but not Intelligence, no doubt because it is only a reflex, a certain expansion or dimension of the Logos, here called Wisdom.

> There are three heads sculptured one in the other and one above the other. One head is the secret hidden Wisdom, which is never unveiled. This mysterious wisdom is the supreme principle of all other wisdom. Above this first head is the Ancient (Whose name be sanctified!), the most mysterious of all the mysteries. Finally comes the head which dominates all the other heads, a head which is not a head. No one knows or can know what that head contains, for it eludes the learned and the ignorant. Hence, the Ancient (Whose name be sanctified!) is called No-Thing (Ayn).

Here we have unity in being, and trinity in intellectual manifestations or thought—exactly our summation.

Sometimes the terms or, if one wishes, the persons, of this trinity are represented as three successive and absolutely necessary phases of existence as well as of thought, or—to use an expression accepted in Germany—as a logical process which at the same time codifies the generation of the world. Whatever astonishment this may excite, it cannot be contradicted. The following lines confirm it:

> Behold thought is the principle of all that is; as such it is at first ignored and confined within itself. When thought begins to spread, it arrives to dwell with spirit; at that point, it takes the name of intelligence and is not, as before, confined within itself. The spirit or mind itself develops in the very bosom of the mysteries by which it is surrounded, and a voice goes forth which is the union of all the heavenly choirs; the voice speaks distinctly and in clear words, for it comes from the spirit. But on reflection it will be found that thought, Intelligence, this voice, and this word are one and the same thing; that thought is the beginning of all that is, and that there can be no break in it. Thought itself is bound to Non-Bĕing (Ayn), and is never parted from it. That is the meaning of the words: Jehovah is One and His name is One.

Here is another passage where the same idea is easily recognized, in a more original and apparently more ancient form:

> The name which signifies 'I Am' shows the union of all that is, the degree where all the ways of wisdom are as yet hidden and united at one place and cannot as yet be distinguished one from another. But when a line of demarcation is established, when it is intended to designate

> the mother bearing all things in her womb and about to bring them forth in order to reveal the supreme name, then, speaking of Himself, God says: 'I Who am.' Finally, when all has been well developed and has left the maternal womb, when everything is in its place, then to describe the particular life, as well as existence, God calls himself Jehovah or 'I Am that I am.' These are the mysteries of the holy name revealed to Moses; no other man shared this knowledge with him.

The system of the Kabbalah does not, therefore, rest solely on the principle of emanation or upon the unity of substance. As we see, the Kabbalists went further. They taught a doctrine very similar to that which the metaphysicians of Germany now regard as the glory of our time. The Kabbalists believed in the absolute identity of thought and existence; consequently, the world could be nothing but the expression of ideas, or of absolute forms of intelligence; in short, they suggest a union of Plato and Spinoza. To buttress this important fact and at the same time show that the most learned of the modern Kabbalists have remained true to the traditions of their predecessors, we quote a very remarkable passage from the commentaries of Cordovera:

> The three first Sefiroth—to wit: the Crown, Wisdom and Intelligence—should be regarded as one and the same thing. The first represents knowledge or science, the second he who knows, and the third that which is known. For the knowledge of the Creator is not like that of His creatures, for whom knowledge is distinct from the subject of knowledge, and depends upon objects which in turn are distinct from the subject. This differentiation is designated by the following three terms: thought, that which thinks, and the thing thought of. The Creator, on

> the other hand, is in Himself knowledge, He who knows, and that which is known. In fact, His manner of knowing does not consist in applying His thought of things outside of Him; rather, it is by understanding and knowing Himself that He knows and perceives all that is. Nothing exists that is not one with Him and that He does not find in His own substance. He is the archetype of all being, and all things exist in Him in their purest and most complete forms; so that the perfection of creatures is inherent in this very existence by which they were united to the source of their being, and in measure as they recede from that source, they fall away from that perfect and sublime state. It is thus that all manner of existence in this world have their form in the Sefiroth, and the Sefiroth have their form in the source from which they emanate.

The seven remaining attributes, which the modern Kabbalists call the Sefiroth of the Construction, undoubtedly because they more immediately serve to edify the world, develop, like the preceding ones, in the form of trinities; in each, two extremes are united by a middle term. From divine thought, when it is most completely revealed, proceed two opposite principles, one active or male, the other passive or female.

In Grace or Mercy is to be found the male principle; the female is represented by Judgment. But it is easily seen from the part played by the two principles in the system as a whole that this Grace and Judgment are not to be taken literally; we are dealing with what we should call the expansion and contraction of the will. In fact, it is from the former that the male soul springs, and from the latter the female soul. These two attributes are also called the "two arms of God"; one gives life, the other death. Were they separated, the world could not subsist; it is even impossible for them to act separately, for in the original formulation, there is no judgment without mercy; they also combine in a common center, Beauty, whose material symbol is the breast or the heart.

The beautiful is considered as the expression and result of all moral qualities, or as the sum of all that is good. But the next three attributes are purely dynamic—that is to say, they represent the Deity as the cause, as the universal force, and as the generative principle of all beings. The first two, representing the male and the female principle in this new sphere, are called, in conformity with the Holy Scriptures, Triumph and Glory. It would be difficult to fix the meaning of the two words were they not followed by this definition: "By the words Triumph and Glory we understand measure, multiplication and force; for all the forces in the universe spring from their midst; hence, these two Sefiroth are called the hosts of the Eternal."

Triumph and Glory combine in a common principle, ordinarily represented by the organs that denote the generative element, or the source, the root of all that is. Hence, it is called the Formation or Foundation (Y'sod). "All things," reads the text, "will re-enter the Foundation from which they issued. All the marrow, all the sap, all power is gathered in that place. All existing forces issue from it by the organ of generation." These three attributes also form one face, one aspect of the divine nature, represented in the Bible by the God of Hosts. As to the last of the Sefiroth, or Kingdom (Malkuth), all Kabbalists agree that it does not express any new attribute, but simply the harmony which eixsts between all the other attributes and their absolute rule over the world.

Thus the ten Sefiroth which in their entirety form the Heavenly or Ideal Man called by modern Kabbalists the "world of emanation," are divided into three classes; each class shows us the deity in a different aspect, but always in the form of an indivisible trinity. The first three Sefiroth are purely intellectual or metaphysical. They express the absolute identity of existence and thought, and form what modern Kabbalists have called the "intelligible world." The next three Sefiroth have a moral character. On the one hand, they conceive God as the identity of kindness and wisdom; on the other hand, they show us that the source of beauty and magnificence is in kindness, or rather in the supreme good. They have therefore been named Virtues, or the "world of feeling" in the loftiest sense of the word. Finally, the last of these attributes teaches that the Universal Province, the Supreme Architect, is also the Absolute Force, the All-Powerful Cause, and that this Cause is at the same time the generating element of all that is. These last Sefiroth constitute the "natural world," or nature in its essence and principle.

How and in what terms these different aspects are brought back to unity and consequently to a supreme trinity, the following passage indicates:

> To understand a holy unity, examine the flame rising from a fireplace or from a lighted lamp. We see at first two kinds of light, one glistening white and one black or blue. The white light is above and rises in a straight line, the black or blue light is beneath and appears to be the source of the white; yet the two lights are so closely united that they form one single flame. But the source formed by the blue or black light is, in turn, attached to the wick under it. The white light never changes, it always remains white; but several shades are distin-

> guishable in the lower light. Moreover, the lower light moves in two opposite directions; above, it is connected to the white light, and below, it is attached to the burning matter; this matter continually consumes itself and rises toward the upper light. It is thus that all that is, reunites with the one unity.

To dispel all doubt as to the meaning of this allegory, we may add that it is found, almost literally reproduced, in another part of the *Zohar* to explain the nature of the human soul, which also forms a trinity—a feeble image of the supreme trinity.

This last trinity, which explicitly comprises all the others and sums up the entire theory of the Sefiroth, plays a most important role in the *Zohar*. Like the preceding trinities, it is represented by three terms, each of which has already been represented as the highest manifestation of one of the lower trinities. Crown represents the metaphysical attributes; Beauty, the moral attribute; Kingdom the inferior attributes. But what is meant by Crown? It is the substance, the one and absolute being. What is Beauty? It is, the *Idra Zuta* expressly says, "the highest expression of moral life and moral perfection." As an emanation from Intelligence and Mercy it is often compared to the Orient, to the sun whose light is reflected equally by all earthly objects and without which all would return to darkness; in a word, it is the ideal.

Finally, what is Kingdom? It is the permanent and immanent action of all the Sefiroth combined, the actual presence of God in the Creation. This idea is fully expressed by the word *Shekinah,* one of the surnames of Kingdom. The true terms of this new trinity are, accordingly, the absolute, the ideal, and the immanent face; or substance, thought, and life; that is, the uniting of thought with object. They constitute what is called "the middle column," because in all the figures customarily used to represent the Sefiroth, they are placed in the center, one above another, in the form of a vertical line or column. As may be expected, these three terms also become so many "faces" or symbolical manifestations. Crown does not change its name; it is always the Long Face, the Ancient of Days, the Ancient Whose name be sanctified. Beauty is the Holy King or simply the King and the Shekinah, the divine presence in things, is the *Matrona*, or Queen.

If Beauty is compared to the sun, Matrona is compared to the moon, because the moon borrows all the light by which it shines from a higher place, just a degree above her. In other words, real existence is only a reflection or image of ideal beauty. Matrona is called Eve for, says the text, "Eve is the mother of all things, and everything that exists here below nurses at her breast and is blessed through her." The King and Queen, commonly called the "two faces," together form a pair whose task is constantly to pour forth new favors on the world, and through their union to continue, or rather to perpetuate, the work of the Creation. But the mutual love which impels them to this creation moves in two ways and consequently produces two species of fruit.

Sometimes love comes from above, going from husband to wife and thence to the entire universe; that is to say, existence and life, originating in the depths of the intelligible world, tend to multiply more and more in the objects of nature. But sometimes love takes a contrary course; rising from below, it moves from wife to husband, from the real world to the ideal world, from earth to heaven, and returns to the bosom of God those beings with some claim to the right of return.

The *Zohar* itself offers an example of these two modes of generation, in the circle traveled by holy souls. The soul, in its purest essence, has its root in Intelligence. We speak here of the Supreme Intelligence, where the forms of being begin to be differentiated from each other, and which is really the universal soul. From there, if it is to be a male soul, it passes through the principle of grace or expansion; if it is a female soul, it impregnates itself with the principle of judgment or concentration. Finally, it is brought forth into our world by the union of the King and Queen who, as the text reads, "are to the generation of the soul, what man and woman are to the generation of the body." By this route the soul descends to earth.

In this manner the soul returns to the bosom of God: When, adorned with all the virtues, it has fulfilled its mission and is ripe for heaven, it rises of its own impulse, by the love it inspires as well as experiences; with the soul rises the last degree of emanation or real existence, which is thus brought in harmony with the ideal form. The King and Queen unite again, impelled by another cause and for another purpose. "In this way," says the *Zohar,* "life is drawn simultaneously from above and below. The source is renewed and the sea, always refilled, distributes its waters to every place." The union may take place accidentally while the soul is still chained to the body. But here we touch upon ecstasy, mystic rapture, and the dogma of reversibility, of which we shall speak later.

Our exposition of the Sefiroth would be incomplete without mention of the figures which have been used to depict them. There are three principal figures, of which two at least are sanctioned by the *Zohar*. One shows the

Sefiroth in the form of ten concentric circles, or rather nine circles traced around a point which is their common center. The other represents the Sefiroth as the human body. The Crown is the head; Wisdom, the brain; Intelligence, the heart; the trunk and breast—that is to say, the middle column—represent Beauty; the arms are the symbols of Grace and Judgment; and the lower parts of the body express the remaining attributes.

It is upon these wholly arbitrary relations, carried to their extreme in the *Tikkunim* (the supplements to the *Zohar*), that the practical Kabbalah and the claim that bodily ills can be cured by the different names of God are for the most part founded. This is not the first time that ideas have been gradually smothered by the crudest symbols and thoughts have been replaced by forms in the decadence of a doctrine.

The last method of representing the ten Sefiroth is to divide them into three groups. To the right, on a vertical line, we see the "expansive" attributes; namely: the Logos or Wisdom, Mercy and Strength. To the left, we find inserted in the same manner, on a parallel line, those which designate resistance or concentration: Intelligence, i.e., the consciousness of the Logos, Judgment and Glory. In the center are the substantive attributes included in the supreme trinity. At the top, above the common level, we read, Crown; at the base, Kingdom.

The *Zohar* often alludes to this figure, which it compares to a tree of which the Ayn Sof is the life and sap; later it was called the "kabbalistic tree." At each step we are reminded of the "column of mercy," the "column of judgment" and the "center column." The same diagram represents the three secondary trinities with horizontal lines. Besides these diagrams, modern Kabbalists have conceived of canals, indicating in a physical form all possible relations and combinations between the Sefiroth. Moses Cordovera tells of an author who drew up six hundred thousand such combinations. These subtleties may be of some interest to the science of calculus, but they are of none to metaphysics.

A strange idea, in still stranger form, merges in the *Zohar* with the doctrine of the Sefiroth. This is the idea of a fall and rehabilitation, in the sphere of the divine attributes—of a creation that failed because God did not descend with it to dwell in it, because He had not yet assumed that intermediary form between Himself and His creatures, of which man is the most perfect expression. These apparently different conceptions have been combined in a single thought which is found, more or less developed, in the Book of Concealment, in the two *Idras*, and in some fragments of less importance.

It is presented in the following strange manner: The Book of Genesis (26:31-40), in naming seven kings of Edom who preceded the kings of Israel, has them die, one after another, to show the order of their succession. It is this text, so alien to such a system of ideas, that the authors of the *Zohar* used as a handle for their belief in a kind of revolution of divine emanation in the invisible world. They interpret the "kings of Israel" to mean the two forms of absolute existence personified in the King and Queen, which represent, when reduced for the sake of our feeble intelligence, the very essence of being. The "kings of Edom" or, as they are also called, the "ancient kings," are the worlds which could neither exist nor be realized until forms were established to serve as intermediaries between creation and the divine essence.

Before the Ancient of Ancients, the most Hidden of the

> Hidden, had prepared the forms of the kings and the first diadems, there was neither limit nor end. So He set about tracing these forms in His own substance. He stretched out a veil, and on this veil He sculpted the kings, tracing their limits and their forms; but they could not exist. Therefore it is written in Scriptures: 'These are the kings that reigned in the land of Edom before there reigned any king over the children of Israel.' This refers to the primitive kings and primitive Israel. All the kings thus formed had names, but they could not exist until He [the Ancient] descended to them and veiled Himself for them.

There can be no doubt that these lines refer to a creation anteceding ours and to worlds preceding ours. Later, the *Zohar* itself states this explicity, and it is also the unanimous belief of all the modern Kabbalists. But why did the ancient worlds disappear? Because God did not dwell in their midst regularly and constantly, or, as the text reads, because God had not come down to them; because He had as yet not shown Himself in a form that permitted Him to be present in the Creation and to perpetuate it by this very union. The worlds which He then produced by a spontaneous emanation from His own essence are like sparks escaping from a hearth which die out the further off they fly.

> Ancient worlds there were which had been destroyed, formless worlds which have been called sparks, for thus it is when striking the iron the blacksmith causes sparks to fly off on all sides. These sparks are the ancient worlds, and these worlds were destroyed and could not exist because the Ancient (Whose name be sanctified!) had as yet not assumed His form and the workman was not yet at his work.

What is the form without which neither duration nor organization of finite beings is possible, which represents the artisan of the divine works, and by which, finally, God communicates and, as it were, reproduces Himself outside of Himself? It is the human form conceived in the most general way, which comprises the moral and intellectual attributes of our nature as well as the conditions of its development and perpetuation—in a word, sexual differentiation which the authors of the *Zohar* relate to the soul as well as the body. To them this concept of sexual differentiation, or rather, the division and reproduction of the human form, is the symbol of universal life, of a regular and infinite development of existence, of a regular and continuous creation, not only through duration, but also through successive realization of all the possible forms of existence.

We have met the root of this idea before; but here is something more. The gradual expansion of life, existence and divine thought did not begin directly with substance; it was *preceded* by tumultuous, disorderly and even inorganic emanation:

> Why were the old worlds destroyed? Because man was not yet formed. The form of man contains all things, and all things can be maintained by it. As this form did not yet exist, the worlds that preceded it could neither subsist nor maintain themselves. They fell in ruins, until the form of man was established. They were then reborn with it, but under other names.

We will not invoke new passages to demonstrate the sexual distinctions in the ideal man or in the divine attributes; we only wish to note here that this distinction, which is repeated under so many different forms in the *Zohar*, is also given the characteristic name of Balance:

> Before balance was established [says the Book of Concealment], they [the King and Queen, the ideal world and the real world] did not see one another face to face and the first kings died because they could find no substance, and the earth was ruined. . . . Balance was suspended in a place that was not [the primitive naught]; they who were to be weighed did not exist as yet. It is entirely an inner balance, that has no other support but itself and is invisible. This balance carries and will carry everything that is not, that is, and that will be.

The kings of Edom, the ancient worlds, did not entirely disappear. For in the kabbalistic system, nothing comes into existence and nothing perishes in an absolute manner. They only lost their place, which was the actual universe; and when God stepped out of Himself to show Himself again in the form of man, the kings of Edom were resuscitated, came to life again in some way to enter into the general system of Creation under other names. "When the Scriptures say, 'The kings of Edom are dead,' it does not mean that they really died, or that they were totally destroyed; for every sinking down from a previous degree is called death." They really did sink very low, or rather rose but little above nothingness; for they were placed on the last rung of the universe. They represent purely passive existence or, to use the *Zohar* expression, Judgment without Mercy, a place where all is sternness and judgment, or where all is feminine without any masculine principle—that is, a place where everything is resistance and inertia, as in matter.

CHAPTER SEVEN

The Zohar: The Kabbalist View of the World

WHAT WE know of the Kabbalists' theory of divine nature spares us the necessity of dwelling on their conception of the Creation and origin of the world; at bottom, they confuse the two concepts. If God unites in Himself the infinite totality of both thought and existence, nothing can be conceived outside of Him. All that we know, then, whether through reason or experience, is a development or a particular aspect of the Absolute; substance, eternal, inert and distinct from God, is a chimera; and Creation, as ordinarily conceived, is an impossibility. The last inference is clearly acknowledged in these words:

> The indivisible point [the absolute] that had no limits and could not be conceived because of its intensity and purity spread outward to form a tent, which served as a cover for this indivisible point. This tent, although of a light less pure than the indivisible point, was still too brilliant to be looked at; in turn, it spread outward, and this expansion was its garment. Thus, everything comes into existence by an ever-descending motion; thus, finally, it was that the universe took shape.

The Absolute Being and visible nature have but one name, whose meaning is God. From another passage we learn that the voice issuing from the spirit, and which is identical with it in the supreme thought, is really water, air and fire, North, South, East and West, and all the forces of nature. All these elements and forces combine in the voice issuing from the spirit. Matter, finally, considered from the most general point of view, is the lowest part of the mysterious lamp.

Thus, the Kabbalists claim to remain true to the popular belief that it was only by the power of the divine word that the world issued from nothingness. But we know already that "nothing" had quite another meaning for them. In the words of Abraham Dior, one of the commentators of the *Sefer Yetzirah*:

> When it is maintained that all things were called forth from nothingness, nothingness in its proper sense is not what it meant, for being can never come out of non-being. Rather, what is meant is the Non-Being that cannot be conceived either through its cause or through its essence; in short, it is the Cause of Causes. It is what we call the primitive Non-Being, anteceding the universe; not only material objects, but also Wisdom, on which the world was founded. To inquire after the essence of

> Wisdom and how it coheres in Non-Being or in the Supreme Crown, is to ask an unanswerable question, for there is no differentiation and no manner of existence in Non-Being. Nor can we understand how Wisdom is united with life.

All Kabbalists, ancient and modern, thus explain the dogma of the Creation. But, consistent, they also admit the second part of the adage: *ex nihilo nihil* (nothing can come from nothing). They have no more belief in absolute annihilation than in Creation as commonly understood.

> Nothing [says the *Zohar*] is lost in the world, not even the vapor that issues from our mouths. Like everything else, it has its place and its destination, and the Holy One, blessed be He, has it concur with His works. Nothing falls into a void, not even the words and voice of man, for all things have their place and their destination.

These words were spoken by an unknown old man in the presence of several disciples of Yohai who must have recognized one of the most esoteric articles of their faith, for they hastened to interrupt:

> Oh, what have you done, old man? Would it not have been better to keep silent? For now, there you are, carried away on an immense sea without sail or mast! Do you want to rise? You cannot. And if you should descend, a bottomless abyss awaits you.

They cited the example of their master, who, at all times reserved in expression, never ventured upon the sea without providing for a safe return—that is to say, he hid his thoughts under the veil of allegory. Later, however, the same principle is stated with complete candor:

> All things of which this world consists, the spirit as well as the body, will return to the principle and the root from which they came. He is the beginning and the end of all degrees of Creation; all degrees are marked with His seal, and he can be designated only by unity. He is *one* despite the innumerable forms with which He is invested.

If God is at one and the same time the cause and the substance, or, as Spinoza would express it, the "immanent cause of the universe," it necessarily follows that the universe is a masterpiece of supreme perfection, wisdom and goodness. To convey this idea the Kabbalists made use of a very original expression, which several of the modern mystics, including Boehm and Saint Martin, have frequently employed. They call nature a "blessing," considering it very significant that the Hebrew letter, *beth,* with which Moses began the story of the Creation (Breshith) is also the first letter in the word "blessing" (Brakah). Nothing is absolutely bad; nothing is accursed forever—not even the archangel of evil or the venomous beast (*havya besha*), as he is sometimes called. There will come a time when he will recover his name and his angelic nature.

Besides, here on earth, wisdom is no less visible than goodness, since the universe was created by the divine word and is itself nothing but this word. Now, in the mystical language of the *Zohar* it means, as we have already learned, that the articulated expression of divine thought is the totality of all the individual beings that exist in potential in the eternal forms of supreme wisdom.

But none of the quoted passages is of greater interest than the following:

> The Holy One, blesed be He, had already created and destroyed several worlds before He decided to create the world we live in; and when that last act was about to be accomplished, all the creatures of the universe and everything that was to be in the world—at whatever time they were to exist—were present before God in their real form before becoming a part of the universe. It is in this sense that we should understand the words of Ecclesiastes: 'That which is hath been long ago, and that which is to be hath already been.' The entire lower world was created in the likeness of the higher world. All that exists in the higher world appears like an image in this lower world; yet all this is but One.

From this exalted belief, which we meet in all the great systems of metaphysics, the Kabbalists drew an inference which leads to mysticism. They imagined that everything which strikes our senses has a symbolic meaning; that phenomena and the most material forms can teach us what transpires in divine thought or in human intelligence. They believed that all that emanates from the mind must manifest itself and become visible outside of it. This concept also leads to belief in a celestial alphabet and physiognomy. This is how they speak of the celestial alphabet:

> Throughout the heavens that surround the world, there are figures and signs by means of which we may discover the most profound secrets and mysteries. These figures are formed by the constellations and stars which are a subject of contemplation and a source of mysterious pleasure for the wise. Anybody who has to set out on a journey the first thing in the morning need only rise at daybreak and look attentively toward the East. He will see something like letters heading towards the

> heavens, one stepping up, another, down. These brilliant shapes are the letters with which God created heaven and earth; they form His mysterious and holy name.

Such ideas may seem unworthy of a place in a serious work, but we should be false to historic truth were we to make known the most brilliant and best-founded thoughts of the system contained in the *Zohar,* while carefully eliminating all that may offend intellectual habits. We have often seen vain illusions of this kind fostered by the same principle—and they were not always the product of the weakest minds. Plato and Pythagoras came close to being counted among them. On the other hand, all the great representatives of mysticism, all those who saw in external nature only a living allegory, adopted the theory of numbers and ideas, each according to his intellectual capacity.

That the Kabbalists accepted physiognomy as well—its name was already known in the time of Socrates—is also a consequence of their general system of metaphysics, or, if we may make use of modern philosophical language, it was by virtue of an *a priori* judgment:

> According to the teachings of the masters of esoteric science, physiognomy does not consist of outwardly manifested features, but on features mysteriously traced in the depth of our inner self. The external features vary according to the form imprinted on the inner face of the spirit. The spirit alone produces all the physiognomies known to the sages, and it is through the spirit that they have a meaning. When souls and spirits come out of Eden (as Supreme Wisdom is often called), they all have definite forms, later reflected in the face.

A large number of detailed observations, some of which

are still credible, follow. For instance: a broad, convex forehead is the sign of a profound and active mind and rare intelligence; a broad flat forehead denotes insanity and stupidity; a flat forehead terminating in a point and compressed at the sides is an unfailing indication of a very limited mind, often combined with unbounded vanity. Finally, all human faces may be traced to four primary types which they approach or depart from according to the rank the souls hold in the intellectual and moral order. These archetypes are the four figures which occupy Ezekiel's mysterious chariot—that is to say, the figures of man, the lion, the ox and the eagle.

It seems to us that the demonology adopted by the Kabbalists is only a personification reflecting the different degrees of life and intelligence which they perceived throughout nature. The belief in demons and angels had long before taken root in the mind of the people, like an entertaining mythology, as it were, alongside the severe dogma of the divine unity. Why then should they not make use of it to veil their ideas on the relations of God to the world, as they made use of the dogma of the Creation to teach the contrary, or as they made use of the words of the scriptural text to raise themselves above the divine word and religious authority?

We have not found an entirely clear-cut text in support of this opinion, but there are several reasons which make it very probable. First of all, the three principal fragments of the *Zohar*, and the two *Idras* and the Book of Concealment, never make mention of the celestial or infernal hierarchy which seems to have been only a memento of the Babylonian captivity. Then, when angels are spoken of in other parts of the *Zohar*, they are represented as beings much inferior to man, as forces of unchanging blind impulses. For example:

> God animated every part of the firmament with a particular spirit; immediately all the celestial hosts were formed and stood before Him. This is the meaning of the Writ (Ps. 33:6): 'By the word of the Lord were the heavens made.' All the higher, holy spirits, who perform His errand, issue from one place, the souls of the just (issue) from two degrees which unite into one; therefore they rise higher, and their degrees are higher.

Even the Talmudists, despite their adherence to the letter of Scriptures, subscribe to the same principle: "The just," they say, "are greater than the angels."

We shall better understand what was meant by the spirits which animate all celestial bodies and elements of the earth, if we study their names, and the functions attributed to them. First, let us exclude the purely poetical personifications—all the angels with names representing a moral quality or a metaphysical abstraction. For instance, good and bad desires are always represented as real personages; then there are the angels of purity (Tahariel), mercy (Rahmiel), justice (Tzadkiel) and deliverance (Peda-el) and the famous Raziel, the angel of secrets, who watches with a jealous eye over the mysteries of kabbalistic wisdom. Moreover, it is a principle recognized by all Kabbalists and connected with their general system of beings that the angelic hierarchy begins only in the third world, the World of Formation, the place occupied by the planets and celestial bodies.

Now, the chief of the invisible militia is the angel Metatron, so called because his place is immediately below the throne of God; he alone constitutes the World of

Creation, or the world of pure spirits. His task is to maintain unity, harmony and the movement of the spheres—the very task of that blind and infinite force which, at times, has been substituted for God under the name of Nature. The myriads of subordinates under Metatron's command are divided into ten categories, undoubtedly in honor of the ten Sefiroth. These subaltern angels are to the different divisions of nature, to every sphere and to every individual element, what their chief is to the entire universe. Thus, one presides over the movements of the earth, another over the movements of the moon, and so on for all the celestial bodies. One is called the angel of fire (Nuriel), another the angel of light (Uriel), a third presides over the course of the seasons, a fourth over vegetation. In short, all the products, forces and phenomena of nature are represented in the same way.

The purpose of this allegory becomes evident when the infernal spirits are considered. We have already called attention to the general name given to all the forces of this order. The demons, according to the Kabbalists, are the grossest and most imperfect forms, the "shells" of existence; in short, everything that denotes absence of life, intelligence and order. Like the angels, they form ten Sefiroth, ten degrees where darkness and impurity grow more and more dense, like in Dante's circles.

The first, or rather the first two degrees, represent the state of the world as depicted in Genesis before the work of the six days of Creation; that is to say, there is an absence of all visible form and organization. The third degree is the source of darkness, the same darkness which in the beginning covered the face of the abyss. Then follow the seven tabernacles or so-called Hell, a systematic outline of all the disorders of the moral world and the torments they cause. There we see every passion of the human heart, every vice and weakness, personified in a demon who becomes the tormentor of those led astray by these faults. In one tabernacle, lust and seduction; in a second, anger and violence; in another, gross impurity, the demon of solitary debauches; in still others, crime, envy, idolatry and pride.

The seven infernal tabernacles are divided and subdivided, *ad infinitum;* for every kind of perversity there is a kind of special kingdom, the abyss gradually unfolding in all its depth and immensity. The supreme chief of this world of darkness, who bears the scriptural name of Satan, the Kabbalah calls Samael—that is to say, the angel of poison or death. The *Zohar* states positively that the angel of death, evil desire, Satan, and the serpent which seduced the first mother are all one and the same. Samael is also given a wife, who is the personification of vice and sensuality, for she is called chief "prostitute," or mistress of debauches. But ordinarily they are combined in a single symbol, simply called the beast.

Reducing this theory of demons and angels to its simplest and most general terms, we find that the Kabbalists recognized in each object of nature, and consequently in all nature, two very distinct elements. One is an inner incorruptibility which reveals itself to the intelligence exclusively, and which is the spirit, life or form. The other, purely external and material, has been made the symbol of degradation, malediction and death. The ancient Kabbalists may have thought, in the words of the philosopher Spinoza: "*Omnia, quamvis diversis gradibus, animata tamen sunt*" (All things, no matter how different in grade, are animated).

CHAPTER EIGHT

The Zohar: The Kabbalist View of the Human Soul

It is mainly because of the high rank the Kabbalists assign man that they recommend themselves to our interest and that the study of their system assumes great importance for the history of philosophy as well as of religion. "For dust thou art, and unto dust shalt thou return," says Genesis (3:19). This curse is followed by neither a definite promise of a better future nor mention of the soul which is to return to God when the body mingles with the earth. The author of Ecclesiastes has bequeathed the following strange comparison to posterity: "For that which befalleth the sons of men befalleth beasts; even one thing befalleth them; as the one dieth, so dieth the other" (Eccles. 3:19).

The Talmud sometimes expresses itself quite poetically on the rewards that await the just. It represents them as seated in the celestial Eden, heads wreathed with light, enjoying the divine glory. But the Talmud endeavors rather to humble than to ennoble human nature in general.

> Whence come you? From a fetid drop. Whither go you? To a place of dust, defilement and worms. And before whom are you some day to vindicate yourself and give account of your actions? Before the King of Kings, before the Holy One Whose name be praised!

Such are the sayings attributed to the oldest and most honored leaders of the talmudic school.

In quite different language, the *Zohar* speaks of our origin, future destiny, and relations with the Divine Being:

> Man is both the summary and the highest expression of Creation; hence, he was not created until the sixth day. As soon as man appeared, everything was completed, the higher world as well as the lower, for all is summed up in man; he unites all form.

But he is not only the image of the world, of the universality of beings, including the absolute; he is also, and above all, the image of God, considered in the totality of His infinite attributes. Man is the divine presence on earth, Celestial Adam, departing from the deepest primitive darkness, produced terrestrial Adam:

> Do not think that man is but flesh, skin, bones and veins; far from it! What really makes man is his soul; and the things we call skin, flesh, bones and veins are but a garment, a cloak; they do not constitute man. When man departs this earth, he divests himself of all the veils that conceal him. Yet, the different parts of the body conform to the secrets of the supreme wisdom. The skin represents the firmament, which extends everything and covers everything, like a cloak. The flesh recalls the evil side of the universe [the purely external and tangible element]. The bones and veins represent the celestial chariot, the forces that exist within, the servants of God. However, all this is but a cloak; for the deep mystery of celestial man is within. Celestial Adam is as spiritual as terrestrial man, and everything happens below as it does on high. Therefore it is written in Scriptures: 'And God created man in His image.' Yet, as different figures formed by the stars and planets in the firmament that envelops us betoken hidden matters and profound mysteries—so do the figures and lines on the skin which encompasses the human body and are the body's stars and planets. All these signs have a hidden meaning and are the objects of attention of wise men who know how to read the face of man.

The most ferocious animal trembles before the unique power of man's external form because of the intelligence and grandeur that are reflected in his features. To protect him from the rage of the lions, says the *Zohar,* the angel sent Daniel nothing but his own face, or the authority experienced through looking like a pure man. But, it adds, this advantage vanishes as soon as man degrades himself through sin and neglect of duty.

When considered as such—that is to say, from the point of view of the soul, and compared to God before He became visible in the world—the human being by virtue of his unity, his substantial identity and his threefold nature, unreservedly recalls the supreme trinity. For the human being consists of the following elements: (1) a spirit which represents the highest degree of his existence; (2) a soul which is the seat of good and evil, of good and evil desires—in short, of all moral attributes; and (3) a coarser spirit which is closely related to the body and is the direct cause of the lower movements—that is, the actions and instincts of animal life.

To understand how these three principles, or rather these three degrees of human existence, are united in one being despite the gap separating them, we return to the comparison previously referred to in describing the divine attributes, whose seed is in the Book of Formation. There are a great many passages about these three souls; we choose the following because of its lucidity:

> In these three elements, the spirit, the soul and the life of the senses, we find a true picture of what transpires on high; for all three make up but a single being, wherein all is joined in unity. The life of the senses has no light of its own; hence it is intimately linked to the body, which it furnishes with pleasures as well as the nourishment it needs. We may apply the words of the sage: 'She giveth food to her household, and a portion to her maidens' (Prov. 21:15). The house is the body that is nourished, and the maidens are the members of the body who obey. Above the life of the senses soars the soul, which subdues the senses, rules them and supplies them with as much light as they need. Thus, the animal principle is the seat of the soul. Finally, above the soul soars the spirit, by which, in turn, it is ruled and which illumines it with the light of life. The soul is illumined by this light and is entirely dependent upon the spirit. After

> death, the soul finds no rest, and the gates of Eden are closed to it until the spirit ascends to its source, towards the Ancient of Ancients, to be replenished by Him for eternity; for the spirit always ascends to its source.

Each of these three souls, as might be anticipated, has its source in a different degree of the divine existence. The supreme wisdom, also called the Celestial Eden, is the only source of the spirit. The soul, according to all the commentators on the *Zohar*, springs from the attribute which unites within itself Judgment and Mercy, that is to say, Beauty. And lastly, the animal principle which never rises above this world, is based on the attributes of strength summarized in the Kingdom.

In addition to these three elements, the *Zohar* recognizes still another, extraordinary, element. It is the external form of man, conceived as a being separate from, and anterior to, the body—in short, the *idea* of the body, but with the individual traits which distinguish each one of us. This idea descends from heaven and becomes visible at the moment of conception:

> At the moment of earthly union, the Holy One, praised be His name, sends down a human-like form which bears the imprint of the divine seal. This form is present at the act of which we spoke, and if we were permitted to see what goes on at the time, we would notice above its head an image resembling a human face; this image is the model after which we are procreated. Procreation cannot take place until this form has been sent by the Lord, until it descends and hovers over our head, for it is written in Scriptures: 'And God created man in His image.' It is this image which receives us first when we come into this world; it develops with us while we grow,

> and accompanies us when we leave the earth. Its source is in heaven. When the souls are about to leave their celestial abode, each of them appears before the Supreme King invested with a sublime form engraved with the traits that are to mark it in this world. The image then emanates from this sublime form; the third from the soul, it precedes us to earth and awaits our arrival from the moment of conception; it is always present at the conjugal union.

Modern Kabbalists call this image the "individual principle."

Some Kabbalists, finally, have introduced into their psychology a fifth principle, called the "vital spirit." The home of this principle is the heart, and it presides over the combination and organization of the material elements. It differs from the principle of animal life and the life of the senses, as the vegetative or nutritive soul differs from the sensitive soul in the philosophy of Aristotle and the scholastics. This opinion is based upon an allegorical passage in the *Zohar,* which says that every night, as we sleep, our soul ascends to heaven to render an account of the day's work; during that time the body is animated only by a breath of life which has its home in the heart.

However, these last two elements—the individual principle and the vital spirit—are not part of our spiritual existence, which is entirely contained in the intimate union of the soul and spirit. The temporary union of these two higher principles with the sense principle—that is to say, life itself—which chains them to earth, is not considered a misfortune. Unlike Origenes and the gnostic schools, the Kabbalah does not regard life as a Fall or an Exile, but as a means for education and a beneficial trial.

According to the Kabbalists, the soul has a need, inherent in its finite nature, to play a part in the universe and to contemplate the spectacle offered by Creation, in order to attain awareness of itself and its origin; and to return without becoming entirely identified with it, to that inexhaustible source of light and life called divine thought.

Moreover, the spirit cannot descend without at the same time raising the two lower principles and even matter, which is to be found further down. Human life, when completed, is therefore a kind of reconciliation between the two extreme expressions of universal existence: between the ideal and the real, between form and matter or, as stated in the Kabbalah, between the King and Queen:

> The souls of the just are, first and foremost, powers and servants from above. And were you to ask why they descend to this world from such a lofty position and wander from their source, I shall answer with the following parable: 'A king had a son who was sent to the country to be reared until he should be sufficiently grown and instructed in the habits of his father's palace. When the father was informed that the education of his son was completed, he sent for the queen, his son's mother, to celebrate his return; then he took his son into his palace to rejoice in his company.'
>
> The Holy One (blessed be His name!) also has a son from the Queen; this son is the superior and holy soul. He sends him to the country, i.e., into this world, to grow up and be initiated in the usage of the royal palace. When the King is informed that His son has reached maturity and that the time has come to take him into His palace, He invites the Queen to the celebration.

> The soul never really leaves the earth except in company with the Queen, who conducts it to the King's palace, where it is to live forever. Yet the inhabitants of the country always weep when the King's son leaves them. But, if there be a clear-sighted man among them, he reprimands the people: 'Why do you cry? Is he not the son of the King? Is it not right that he leave you to go live in his Father's palace?' Thus Moses, who knew the truth, spoke to the weeping countryfolk. 'Ye are the children of the Lord your God, ye shall not cut yourselves . . . for the dead.' If all the just could know this, they would welcome the day when they must quit this world. And is it not the height of glory when the Queen [the Shekinah or Divine Presence] descends among them, when they are admitted to the palace of the King and enjoy His delights forever?

In these relations between God, nature and the human soul, we again find the same type of trinity which we have met so often before, and to which the Kabbalists seem to have attached a logical importance of greater dimension than the exclusive sphere of religious ideas would permit.

But it is not only from this point of view that human nature is in the image of God. It also includes at all stages of its development the two generative principles, of which the trinity, with the aid of a middle term flowing from their union, is only the result or the most complete expression. Celestial Adam being the consequence of a male and female principle, the same had to hold for terrestrial man, and not only for his body, but above all, his soul.

> Every form in which the male and female principle is not to be found [says the *Zohar*] is not a superior or

> complete form. The Holy One, blessed be He, does not establish His abode where these two principles are not perfectly united; the blessing comes down only where this union exists, as we learn from the following words: 'He blessed *them* and called *their* name (Adam) on the day they were created (Gen. 5:2); for the name of Man can be given only to a man and a woman who are united into one being.'

Just as the soul was in the beginning completely merged with the supreme intelligence, so the two halves of the human being, each of which comprises all the elements of our spiritual nature, were joined together before they came into this world, whither they were sent only to report and to unite anew in the bosom of God. This thought is nowhere expressed as clearly as in the following fragment:

> Every soul and every spirit before coming into this world is composed of a male and a female united in one being. Descending to earth, these two halves separate and go off to animate different bodies. At the time of marriage, the Holy One, blessed be He, Who knows all souls and spirits, unites them as before, and they become again a single body and a single soul.... But this union is consistent with the actions of man and the ways he has traveled. If he is pure and behaves piously, he will enjoy a union exactly like the one that preceded his birth.

The author of these lines may have heard of Plato's hermaphrodites; for the name of these imaginary beings are well known in the ancient traditions of the Hebrews. But how inferior to the Kabbalists was the Greek philosopher on this point! The question under consideration here, and the very principle by which it is solved, is worthy of a great metaphysical system. For if man and woman are two beings equal in their spiritual nature and by the absolute laws of morality, they are far from being alike in the natural direction of their faculties; we have reason to agree with the *Zohar* that sexual distinction obtains no less for the soul than for the body.

The belief just expounded is inseparable from the dogma of pre-existence, which is already included in the theory of ideas and is even more closely linked to the theory combining existence and thought:

> When the Holy One, praised be He, was about to create the world, the universe was already present in His thought. He then formed the souls which were eventually to belong to man, and they appeared before Him in the very same form they were later to take in the human body. God examined them one by one, and found several which were destined to become corrupt in this world. When the time came, each of the souls was summoned before God, Who said: 'Go to this or that part of the earth and animate such and such a body.' The soul replied: 'O Master of the Universe, I am happy in this world and do not want to leave it for another where I shall be exposed to contamination.' The Holy One, blessed be He, then said: 'From the day you were created you were destined for the world to which I send you.' Seeing that it had to obey, the soul sorrowfully took the earthly path and descended among us.

Aong with this idea we find the doctrine of reminiscence expressed very simply in the following passage:

> Just as all the things of this world, in their proper

> form, were present in God's thoughts before the Creation, so before coming into this world did all human souls exist in the presence of God in heaven in the form which they have here below; and all that they learn here, they already knew before coming here.

It is perhaps regrettable that such an important principle has not been developed further and is not accorded more space in the general system. But we must admit that it is expressed quite categorically.

We must be careful, however, not to confound this doctrine of pre-existence with that of moral predestination. With the first, human liberty is entirely impossible; with the second, it is only a mystery which can no more be revealed by pagan dualism or the biblical dogma of Creation, than by belief in absolute unity. This mystery is formally acknowledged by the *Zohar*:

> 'If the Lord,' said Simeon ben Yohai, to his disciples, 'if the Holy One, blessed be He, had not given us the good and the evil desires which Scriptures call light and darkness, there would be neither merit nor guilt for the created man [man proper].' 'But why is it so?' demanded the disciples. 'Would it not be better if there were neither reward nor punishment and man were incapable of sinning or doing evil?' 'No!' answered the master, it is well that man was created as he is, and all that the Holy One, praised be He, did, was necessary. The Law was made for the sake of man; but the Law is a cloak for the Divine Presence (Shekinah). Without man and without the Law, Shekinah would be like a pauper without a cloak to cover himself.'

In other words, the moral nature of man, the idea of good and evil, which cannot be conceived without liberty, is one of the forms in which we are forced to picture the absolute being. True, we have been told previously that God knew, before they came to this world, which souls were to desert Him later on, but His foreknowledge did not hamper their freedom. On the contrary, it dates to this time, and even spirits which have been liberated from the bondage of matter can abuse liberty:

> All those who do evil in this world began their estrangement from the Holy One, praised be He, in heaven; they hastened to the edge of the abyss and anticipated the time of their descent to earth. Such was the condition of the souls before they came among us.

It is for the very purpose of reconciling liberty with the destiny of the soul and of giving man the means of expiating his faults without banishing him forever from the bosom of God, that the Kabbalists adopted and ennobled the Pythagorean dogma of metempsychosis. Like all individual beings, the souls must return to the absolute substance from which they have departed. But to do so they must have developed all perfections, the indestructible germ of which is within them, and through many trials must have attained consciousness of themselves and of their origin. If they have not fulfilled these conditions in a previous life, they begin a second, and afterward a third, life, always moving on to a new condition where the acquisition of the missing virtue depends entirely upon themselves. We can end this exile whenever we wish, but nothing prevents us from continuing it forever.

> All souls [says the text] are subject to the trials of transmigration, and man does not know the ways of the

> Holy One, blessed be He. He does not know that he is called to judgment before entering this world as well as after leaving it. He does not know how many transformations and secret trials he has to pass through, how many souls and spirits enter this world and do not return to the palace of the Heavenly King, and finally that souls undergo revolutions similar to those of a stone shot from a sling. The time has finally come when these secrets must be divulged.

According to St. Jerome, the transmigration of the soul was taught for a long time among the early Christians as an esoteric and traditional doctrine which was to be divulged to only a small number of the elect: *abscondite quasi in foveis viperaum versari, et quasi haereditario malo serpere in paucis.* Origen considered the doctrine to be the only possible explanation of such biblical accounts as the prenatal scuffle between Esau and Jacob, of Jeremiah's appointment while still in his mother's womb, and of a host of other events which would accuse the heavens of iniquity were they not justified by the good or evil actions of a pre-existing life. To remove all doubt as to the origin and true character of this belief, the Alexandrian priest carefully adds that it is not Plato's metempsychosis which is at issue here, but a far different and much loftier theory.

To help us regain heaven, modern Kabbalists have conceived another remedy, offered by divine grace in our weakness. They speculate that since separate souls lack the power to fulfill all the precepts of the Law, God combines them in one life, so that like the blind man and the lame, they may complement each other. Sometimes it is only one of two souls which needs additional virtue and therefore seeks it in the other, better favored, and stronger soul. The latter then becomes like a mother, carrying the weaker soul in its bosom and nourishing it from its own substance, like a woman nursing the fruit of her womb. Whence the term gestation, or impregnation, whose philosophical meaning, if there be one, is hard to guess.

We know that the soul's return to the bosom of God is the end of, as well as the compensation for, all the ordeals of which we have spoken. However, the authors of the *Zohar* did not stop there. To them, the union which causes such inexpressible joy to the Creator as well as to the created is a natural fact, whose principle rests on the very constitution of the soul; in short, they endeavor to explain this doctrine by a psychological system which we find at the bottom of every theory fathered by mysticism. Having separated from human nature the blind force which presides over animal life, which never leaves the earth and consequently plays no part in the destinies of the soul, the *Zohar* distinguishes between two kinds of sentiments and two cognitions. Awe and love make up the first two; direct light and reflected light, or the inner face and other faces, are the expressions ordinarily used to designate the last two.

> The inner face [says the text] receives its light from the supreme light, which shines forever and whose secret can never be divulged. It is an inner face because it comes from a hidden source; but it is also a superior face because it comes from on high. The outer face is but the reflection of that light which emanates directly from on high.

This dual cognition is very often called the "luminous mirror" and the "non-luminous mirror." They are also encountered under these names in the Talmud. When God told Moses that he might see only His back and not His face, He was alluding to these two kinds of cognition, which are represented in the early paradise by the tree of life and the tree of knowledge of good and evil. This is, in short, what we would call nowadays "intuition" and "reflection."

It is worthy of note that the Talmud, when speaking of Moses, also uses the expression "luminous mirror" and "non-luminous mirror"; yet, contrary to the *Zohar,* the Talmud says of Moses that he saw the Deity in the luminous mirror. Of interest, too, is the Orthodox Jewish custom of looking at the fingernails and fingertips when blessing the candle at the end of Sabbath, a custom based upon a *Zohar* passage.

Love and awe, considered from the religious standpoint, are defined in a very remarkable manner:

> Through awe we come to love. One who obeys God out of love has undoubtedly attained the highest degree and in his sanctity is assured of the hereafter. It should not be believed, however, that to serve God through awe is not to serve at all. On the contrary, such homage is very precious, although the union it establishes between the soul and God is not so lofty. There is only one degree more elevated than that of awe, and that is love. Love contains the mystery of the unity of God. It is love that links the higher with the lower degrees; it is love that lifts everything to the level where all must become one. This is also the secret of the words: Hear O Israel, the Lord our God, the Lord is *One.*

Having reached the highest degree of perfection, the soul knows neither reflection nor awe. Its blissful existence, entirely contained in intuition and love, has lost its individual character; uninterested, inactive, unwilling to resume its identity, it can no longer separate itself from divine existence. Here is how, in fact, this kind of existence is represented from the viewpoint of intelligence:

> Behold: when the souls have arrived at the place called the 'treasure of life,' they enjoy that brilliant light whose source is in the highest heaven; the splendor of the light is so great that the souls could not bear it were they not clothed with a cloak of light. This cloak enables them to look into the dazzling hearth, which illuminates life's abode. Moses himself could approach and look at this light only after discarding his earthly robes.

To learn how the soul unites with God through love, listen to the words of the old man whom the *Zohar* rates as the most important figure after Simeon ben Yohai:

> In one of the most mysterious and exalted parts of heaven there is a palace of love. The most profound mysteries are there; all the souls well-beloved by the Celestial King, the Holy One, praised be He, together with the holy spirits with whom He unites in kisses of love. Hence the death of the righteous is referred to as God's kiss.

"This kiss," the text expressly states, "is the union of the soul with the substance from which it springs."

The same principle explains why all the interpreters of mysticism venerate the tender but often profane expressions of the Song of Songs. "My beloved is mine, and I am his," said Simeon ben Yohai before dying, and it is especially noteworthy that this quotation closes Gerson's treatise on mystic theology as well. Notwithstanding the surprise that may be generated by the juxtaposition of this justly celebrated name and that of Fenelon with those that figure in the *Zohar*, we shall have no trouble demonstrating that the *Considerations on Mystic Theology* and the *Explanations of the Maxims of the Saints* contain the same theory of love and contemplation as the Kabbalah.

Here we have the conclusion, which no one has acknowledged as candidly as the Kabbalists. Among the degrees of existence (also called the "seven tabernacles") is one designated the "saint of saints," in which the souls unite with the supreme soul and mutually complete themselves. In this stage, all things return to unity and perfection. Everything unites in a single thought which expands and completely fills the universe. But the foundation of this thought, the light that is hidden within, can never be grasped or known; we may grasp only the thought that emanates from it. In this final state, the creature cannot be distinguished from the Creator. The same thought illumines both; the same will animates both; the soul as well as God commands the universe, and God executes what the soul commands.

To complete this analysis we must show in a few words the opinion the Kabbalists have of a traditional dogma which, while of secondary consideration in their system, is of the greatest importance in the history of religions. The *Zohar* frequently mentions the Fall and the curse which its disobedience of our first parents brought to humanity. It teaches us that in yielding to the serpent, Adam called down death upon himself, his posterity and all of nature. Before his sin Adam was more powerful and beautiful than the angels. If he had a body at all, it was not of that base matter of which our bodies are made; he shared none of our needs and none of our sensual desires. He was enlightened by a higher wisdom, which the divine messengers of the highest rank were constrained to envy.

We cannot say, however, that this dogma is the same as that of the "original sin." In fact, considering only the posterity of Adam, we are not dealing with a crime which no human virtue is able to expunge, but with a hereditary misfortune, a terrible punishment which extends into the future as well as the present. "The pure man," says the text, "is in himself a true sacrifice, which may serve as atonement; it is because of this that the righteous are the sacrifice and the means of atonement of the universe."

The Kabbalists go so far as to represent the angel of death as the greatest benefactor in the universe: "For, the Law was given to us as a protection against him; on his account the righteous will inherit those sublime treasures which are reserved for them in the life to come." However, this old belief in the fall of man, which is so positively taught in Genesis, is ably set forth in the Kabbalah as a natural fact, like the creation of the soul:

> Before Adam sinned, he obeyed only the wisdom whose light shines from on high; he had as yet not separated himself from the tree of life. But when he yielded to the desire to know the things here below and to descend to them, tempted, he became acquainted with evil and forgot the good; he separated himself from the tree of life. Before Adam and Eve committed the sin, they heard the voice from on high, were in possession of higher wisdom, and retained their sublime and luminous nature. But after their sin, they could not understand even the voice from below.

Before they were beguiled by the subtleness of the serpent, Adam and Eve were not only exempt from the need of a body, but did not even have a body—that is to say, they were not of the earth. Both were pure intelligences, happy spirits like those dwelling in the abode of the elect. This explains the scriptural text where Adam and Eve are represented as nude during their state of innocence. When we are told by the writer of sacred history that God clothed them in tunics of skin, he means that God provided them with bodies and the faculty of sensation, so they might be able to inhabit this world to which they were drawn by an imprudent curiosity or the desire to know good and evil. Here is one of the numerous passages where this idea, adopted by Philo and Origen, is expressed very clearly:

> When our forefather Adam inhabited the Garden of Eden, he was clothed, as all are in heaven, with a garment made of the higher light. When he was driven from the Garden of Eden and was compelled to submit to the needs of this world, what happened? God, the Scriptures tell us, made Adam and his wife tunics of skin and clothed them; for before this they had tunics of light, of that higher light used in Eden. . . . The good actions accomplished by man on earth draw down on him a part of that higher light which shines in heaven. It is this light which serves him as garment when he must enter into another world and appear before the Holy One, Whose name be praised. Thanks to this garment he is able to taste the bliss of the elect and to look into the luminous mirror. That it may be perfect in all respects, the soul has a different garment for each of the two worlds it must inhabit—one for the earthly world and one for the higher world.

On the other hand, we know that death, which is sin itself, is not a universal curse but only self-willed evil; it does not exist for the righteous, who unite with God by a love-kiss; it strikes only the wicked, who leave all hope behind in this world. The dogma of original sin seems to have been adopted by the modern Kabbalists, principally by Isaac Luria. Believing that all souls were born with Adam, and all formed one and the same soul, he regarded them all as equally guilty of the first act of disobedience. But, while showing them thus degraded since the beginning of Creation, Luria accords them the faculty of elevating themselves through their own efforts by fulfilling all the commandments of God. Therefore, the obligation to bring the souls out of this state and to fulfill the precept: "Be fruitful and multiply." Therefore also, the necessity for metempsychosis, for a single lifetime does not suffice for this work of rehabilitation. Even in another form, the soul is always offered the ennoblement of our earthly existence and the sanctification of life as the only means of attaining perfection, the need and the germ of which the soul carries within itself.

It is not part of our plan to pass judgment upon the vast system we have explained. Nor could we do so without profaning the philosophy and religious dogmas, whose mystery is justly respected. To summarize, we find that the Kabbalah, as presented by the *Sefer Yetzirah* and the *Zohar*, is composed of the following elements:

1. By taking all the facts and words of Scripture as symbols, the Kabbalah teaches man to have confidence in himself; it substitutes reason for authority and creates a philosophy in the very bosom and under the protection of religion.

2. For belief in a creative God outside of nature and

eternally inactive notwithstanding His omnipotence, the Kabbalah substitutes the idea of a universal substance, infinite in reality, always active, always thinking, the immanent cause of the universe but not confined by it; to which "to create" means but to think, exist and develop itself.

3. Instead of a purely material world, outside of God, sprung from nothingness and destined to return thither, the Kabbalah recognizes innumerable forms in which the divine substance develops and manifests itself according to invariable laws of thought. Everything exists united in the supreme intelligence before being realized in a sentient form. Therefore, there are two worlds, one intelligible or superior, the other inferior or material.

4. Of all these forms, man is the most exalted, the most complete, and the only one permitted to represent God. Man is the bond and the transition between God and the world, reflecting both in his twofold nature. Like everything else of a finite nature, man is at first part of the absolute substance with which he must reunite some day when he has been prepared by developments to which he is susceptible. But we must distinguish between the absolute form—the universal form of man—and its faint reproduction, the particular man. The first, called "celestial man," is inseparable from divine nature; it is its first manifestation.

Some of these elements serve as a basis for systems which may be looked upon as contemporaneous with the Kabbalah. Others were known at a much earlier time. For the history of human intelligence, it is of great interest to find out whether the esoteric doctrine of the Hebrews is really original, or but a disguised copy.

PART THREE

Philosophic Resemblances to the Kabbalah

CHAPTER NINE

The Kabbalah and the Philosophy of Plato

SOME OF the systems which, because of their own nature or that of the age which gave rise to them, seem likely to have served as basis and pattern for the esoteric doctrine of the Hebrews, are philosophical, some religious. The first category includes the systems of Plato and his unfaithful Alexandrian disciples, and of Philo, not to be confounded with them. Of the religious systems we can at this point mention only Christianity, and that in a general way. None of these grand theories of God and Nature, however, explain the origin of the kabbalistic traditions.

No one will deny that there is a close analogy between the Platonic philosophy and certain metaphysical and cosmological principles taught in the *Zohar* and the Book of Formation. In both we see the Divine Intelligence or the Word shaping the universe according to types contained within Himself before Creation. In both we see numbers serving as intermediaries between ideas—between the supreme concept and the objects which are its incomplete manifestation in the world. In both, finally, we find the dogmas of the pre-existence of souls, of reminiscence and of metempsychosis. These resemblances are so striking that modern Kabbalists have recognized them and, in explanation, made Plato a disciple of Jeremiah, as others have made Aristotle a disciple of Simon the Just. Some scholars, in fact, theorize that Aristotle, while in Palestine with Alexander the Great, saw the works of Solomon, and that these furnished him with the principal elements for his philosophy.

Will anyone dare, however, to conclude from such superficial relationships that the works of the Athenian philosopher inspired the first authors of the Kabbalah? Or, what is more astonishing, that this science of strange origin, born of a heathen mind, was held in such high regard and wrapped in so much mystery by the Mishna? Yet those who hold to this opinion are the very same critics who view the *Zohar* as a mere thirteenth-century invention; they would thus have it appear at a time when Plato was not known—for no one will claim that the scattered citations of Plato in the works of Aristotle, and the caustic criticism accompanying them, can transmit any conception of the Platonic doctrine.

In any case, we cannot accept the actual affiliation of the Kabbalah with the Platonic philosophy. The resemblances first noticed between the two doctrines are soon wiped out by their differences. Plato formally acknowledged two principles: spirit and matter—the intelligent cause and the inert substance; although from what he says, it is hard to have as clear an idea of the second as of the first. The Kabbalists, on the contrary, spurred on by the incomprehensibility of the Creation *ex nihilo* (from nothing), accepted absolute unity as the basis of their system: a God Who is at one and the same time the cause, the substance, and the form of all that is, as well as of all that can be.

Like everyone else, the Kabbalists acknowledge the struggle between good and evil, spirit and matter, power and resistance; but they subordinate this struggle to the absolute principle. They ascribe it to the necessary difference in the generation of things between the finite and the infinite, between all individual existence and its limitation, between the furthest points on the scale of beings. This fundamental dogma, which the *Zohar* sometimes interprets through profoundly philosophical expressions, appears in the *Sefer Yetzirah* in fanciful and rough form; but it is clearly original or, at least, free of Plato's influence. When we compare Platonic theory of ideas with the theory of the Sefiroth, and these two with the inferior forms that flow from them, we find the same distance separating them as separates dualism from absolute unity.

By placing an abyss between the intelligent principle and inert matter, Plato can see in ideas nothing but forms of intelligence—of that supreme intelligence of which our own is but a conditional and limited part. These forms are eternal and incorruptible, like the principle to which they belong; for the forms are themselves the idea and the intelligence, so there can be no intelligent principle without them. In this sense they also represent the essence of things, which cannot exist without form or the imprint of the divine idea. But the forms cannot represent all that exists in the inert principle nor the principle itself. Yet, since the principle exists, and in all eternity, it is necessary that it, too, have its own essence, its distinctive and invariable attributes, although it is subject to all changes.

We deny that Plato meant to describe matter as a simple negotiation—that is to say, the boundary which circumscribes each particular existence. This role he assigns expressly to numbers, the principle of every boundary and of every proportion. But together with numbers and the productive and intelligent cause, he posits the Infinite, which is more or less responsive to that from which things are produced—in short, matter or, to be more exact, substance separated from causality. There are therefore existences, or rather forms of existence — unchangeable modes of being—which are necessarily excluded from the body of ideas. This is not the case with the Sefiroth of the Kabbalah, where matter itself figures. Because they suppose them to be perfectly identical, the Sefiroth present both the forms of existence and of the idea, the attributes of inert substance—that is to say, of passivity or resistance—as forms of intelligent causality.

The Sefiroth are therefore divided into two great classes called, in the metaphysical language of the *Zohar,* "fathers" and "mothers." These two apparently opposite principles, coming from one inexhaustible source—the Infinite—reunite in one common attribute called the "son," whence they separate to reunite in a new form. Hence the trinitarian system of the Kabbalists, which no one can possibly confound with the Platonic trinity.

Different as its foundations were from those of Greek philosophy, the kabbalistic system may claim only relative originality. For absolute originality is exceedingly rare and perhaps never to be found in metaphysics; and it is known that Plato himself does not owe everything to his own genius. Before taking on a character truly worthy of reason and science, all great conceptions of the supreme cause, the first existence and the generation of things appeared first in a more or less crude form. Thus, a tradition which does no harm to the independence and fertility of the philosophical spirit may be acceptable.

Yet, having made this disclaimer, we maintain that the Kabbalists had no direct relationship with Plato. Indeed, if we fancy the Kabbalists to have drawn from the source of the most independent philosophy, to have been nourished by this jesting and pitiless dialectic that puts everything to question, destroying as often as it builds up—if we think that a superficial reading of the "Dialogues" initiated them into all the elegance of the most refined civilization—how are we to understand the irrational, rude, and unbridled imagination in the most important passages of the *Zohar*? Can we explain away the extraordinary description of the white head, those gigantic metaphors mingled with puerile details, the supposition of a secret revelation older than that of Sinai, and finally those incredible efforts, aided by the most arbitrary means, to find their own doctrine in the Holy Scriptures?

In these characteristics we can recognize a philosophy which, springing from the bosom of an eminently religious people, dares not own up to its own audacity, and for its own peace of mind seeks refuge in authority. But we cannot reconcile these characteristics with the perfectly free choice of a strange and independent philosophy which openly avers that it derives its authority, power and enlightenment from reason alone. Moreover, the Jews never disavowed their foreign teachers nor withheld homage from other nations for the knowledge they sometimes borrowed from them; the Talmudists were indeed very scrupulous about mentioning the name of the originator of an opinion. Thus the Talmud tells us that the Assyrians furnished the names of the months and of the angels, as well as the characters which the Jews use to this day in their holy books. Later, when the Greek language began to spread among them, the most venerable teachers of the Mishna spoke of it with admiration.

Finally, in a very remarkable passage we are informed by the *Zohar* itself that the books of the Orient come very close to the Divine Law and to some views taught by the school of Simeon ben Yohai. This ancient wisdom was taught by the patriarch Abraham to the children begotten with his concubine who, according to the Bible, populated the Orient. What could have prevented the authors of the Kabbalah from dedicating a memento to Plato as well? Could they not just as easily as their modern followers have had it that he was schooled by some prophet of the true God? According to Eusebius of Caesarea (264-340), considered the father of church history, this is exactly what Aristobulus of Paneas, Jewish Alexandrian philosopher of the second or third century B.C., did when, after interpreting the Bible in accordance with the philosophy of Plato, he felt no pain in accusing him of having drawn all his knowledge from the books of Moses. The same stratagem was used by Philo against the leader of the Portico, the philosopher Zeno (360-270 B.C.).

We are therefore entitled to the opinion that the origin of the kabbalistic system is not to be found in Platonism.

CHAPTER TEN

The Kabbalah and the Alexandrian School

THE METAPHYSICAL and religious doctrine which we have gathered from the *Zohar* undoubtedly bears a more intimate resemblance to the so-called Neo-Platonic philosophy than it does to pure Platonism. But before indicating what the *Zohar* has in common with Neo-Platonism, are we justified in concluding that the Kabbalah is necessarily its copy? One word would suffice to answer this question, were we content with a superficial critique; for we would have no trouble in establishing that the secret doctrine of the Hebrews existed long before Ammonius Saccas, Plotinus and Porphyrius transformed the aspect of philosophy. But for weighty reasons, we subscribe to the theory that it took the Kabbalah several centuries to develop and establish itself in its ultimate form. A supposition that the Kabbalah borrowed a great deal from the pagan school of Alexandria continues to merit our serious consideration; especially when we bear in mind that after the revolution brought about in the Orient by the Macedonian armies, many Jews adopted the language and civilization of their conquerors.

We must start from the proven fact that the Kabbalah came to us from Palestine, as attested by its close connection with the rabbinical institutions. For the Jews of Alexandria spoke Greek and would never have made use of the popular and corrupt idiom of the Holy Land. Now, what were the relations between these countries and the civilizations they represented, from the time the Neo-Platonic school made its appearance until the middle of the fourteenth century—a period during which Judea witnessed the death of its last schools, its last patriarchs and its last sparks of intellectual and religious life? Had the pagan philosophy penetrated the Holy Land during this interval, one might assume the intervention of the Alexandrian Jews, who for several centuries had been as familiar with the principal monuments of Greek civilization as they were with the holy books—a fact borne out by the Septuagint and the example of Aristobulus.

But the Alexandrian Jews had so little communication with their Palestinian brethren that they completely ignored the rabbinical institutions, which played such a great role in Palestine and which, for more than two centuries before the common era, were deeply rooted there. Scrutinizing the works of Philo, the Book of Wisdom and the last Book of the Maccabees, both of which flowed from an Alexandrian pen, we find no mention of any of the names which, in Judea, were endowed with the most sacred authority—such as the high priest Simon the Just, the last representative of the Great Synagogue, and the revered Tannaim who succeeded him. We never even find an allusion to the famous dispute between Hillel and Shemmai (two great leaders cited in the Mishna who flourished from about 78 to 44 B.C., or before Philo), nor to the various customs which were later collected in the Mishna and attained legal force. In his *Life of Moses,* Philo does not mention an oral tradition, preserved by the Elders of Israel and usually studied with the text of the Scriptures. But this tradition, which may have been invented to intersperse pleasant fables in the life of the Hebrew prophet, has nothing in common with the traditions which form the basis of the rabbinical cult. It reminds us of the Midrashim, those popular, unauthoritative legends which abound in Judaism at every epoch of its history.

The Palestinian Jews, on the other hand, were no better informed of the fate of their scattered brethren in Egypt. They knew only from hearsay of a supposed version of the Septuagint which dates from a much earlier epoch than the one now claiming our attention. They eagerly accepted the fable of Aristeas, whch harmonized so well with their national self-love and inclination to the marvelous. This passage clearly shows not only that the authors of the Talmud did not know the Septuagint (there were supposed to be seventy-two translators), but that because of their ignorance of the Greek language and literature they could not possibly have known it. Indeed, in enumerating the changes made in the text of the Pentateuch by the seventy-two Elders who were especially inspired by the Holy Spirit for that purpose, they point out ten places, of which some never existed, or not the least trace has been found, or in most instances are either ridiculous or impossible.

Not a word is found in the Mishna or the two Gemaras which would be applicable to the philosopher Aristobulus, to Philo, or to the author of the apocryphal books mentioned earlier. Still more surprising is the fact that the Talmud never mentions the Therapeutae, or even the Essenes, although the latter were already well established in the Holy Land during the time of the historian Josephus. Such silence can be explained only by the origin of these two sects and the language they employ for the transmission of their doctrines. Both sects originated in Egypt and probably retained the use of Greek, even on the soil of their religious fatherland. The Talmud's silence, especially with regard to the Essenes, would otherwise be still more inexplicable; for, according to Josephus, these sects were already known during the reign of Jonathan Maccabeus, a century and a half before the Christian era.

If the Jews of Palestine lived in such ignorance of their own brethren, some of whom certainly merited their pride, why should it be supposed that they were informed about events in the equally remote pagan school? We have already said that they held the Greek language in high esteem; but were they sufficiently familiar with it to follow the philosophic trend of their time? We have every reason to doubt this. First of all, we find neither trace nor mention in either Talmud or *Zohar* of any monument of Greek civilization. And how is it possible to understand a language whose works are not known? Next, we learn from Josephus, who himself was born in Palestine and spent most of his life there, that this famous historian required help in writing, or rather, translating his works into Greek. Elsewhere in his works, he expresses himself even more explicitly on this subject, ascribing to his compatriots what he acknowledges about himself; he then adds that the study of languages is looked upon in his country as a profane occupation, worthy rather of slaves than of free people, and that only those who are highly knowledgeable about the religious laws and the Holy Scriptures are held in high esteem and known as savants.

Yet Josephus belonged to one of the most distinguished families in the Holy Land. Of royal blood and priestly rank, none was more fit than he to be an initiate of all the knowledge of his country, religious as well as political. Furthermore, in devoting himself to profane studies, the author of *Jewish Antiquities* and *Jewish War* was not subject to the same scruples as were his compatriots who remained true to their country and their belief.

Even admitting that the Greek language was much more cultivated in Palestine than we have reason to believe, we are still in no position to draw any conclusion regarding the influence of the Alexandrian philosophy; for the Talmud makes a clear distinction between the Greek language and what it calls Greek science. Greek science is one thing, the Greek language another; the former was respected and honored; the latter, execrated. The Mishna, always very terse, as a collection of legal decisions would necessarily be, confines itself to prohibiting the rearing of children in Greek lore, adding that this interdiction was effected during the war with Titus.

The Gemara, though, is more explicit, placing this interdiction at an earlier date:

> The following has been taught us by our masters: During the war that raged between the Hasmonean princes, Hyrcanus laid siege to Jerusalem, and Aristobulus was besieged. Every day a basket full of coins was lowered along the outer wall, and in exchange the animals required for sacrifices were sent up. Now, in the camp of the besieger there was an old man who was familiar with Greek learning. He said: 'As long as your enemies are able to hold divine service, they will not fall into your hands.' The next day the basket full of coins was lowered as usual, but a pig was sent up instead of the sacrificial animal. When the unclean animal was half way up the rampart, it thrust its claws against the wall and the land of Israel trembled for four hundred parasangs around. At that time the curse was pronounced: Cursed be he who raises pigs; cursed be we who imparts Greek learning to his children.

Apart from the fabulous and ridiculous circumstances of the earthquake, this account is of value. The gist is apparently true for it is also found in Josephus. According to him, Hyrcanus' men promised sacrificial animals to the besieged upon receipt of one drachma per head, then made them surrender the money but refused to relinquish the animals. To the Jews this was doubly odious—a violation of an oath to men and a blow against God Himself. When we add the very probable circumstances that in place of the sacrificial animal so impatiently awaited, the priests were confronted in the holy place with an animal which was utterly disgusting to them, then we can see that blasphemy and perjury had reached their peak.

Now then, who was responsible for such a crime? Where are we to look for the first impulse? Surely with those who neglected the Law of God for the wisdom of other nations.

Whether or not this accusation is well founded is of little importance; whether the anathema was pronounced during the Hasmonean war or the war of Titus is of still less importance to us. What does interest us, though, and what seems to be beyond doubt, is that Greek learning was looked upon in Palestine as a source of impiety, constituting a double sacrilege. No sympathy or alliance, therefore, could be established between those who were suspected of Greek learning and the founders or keepers of rabbinical orthodoxy.

It is true that the Talmud also reports—in the name of Rabbi Judah who heard it from an older teacher, Samuel —the following words of Simon, son of Gamaliel, who played such a beautiful part in the Acts of the Apostles: "There were a thousand children in the home of my father; five hundred studied the Law, and five hundred were instructed in Greek learning. Today only myself, here, and the son of my father's brother, in Asia, remain." The Gemara comments: "An exception was made for the family of Gamaliel because it was close to the royal court." Let us note, besides, that the entire passage is less trustworthy than the previous one; here, it is no longer a question of general tradition but of simple hearsay on the part of an individual witness who is already far removed from his source. Gamaliel's character, as depicted by tradition, is distinguished from that of the other teachers of the Law by his very attachment to the Orthodox wing of Judaism, and the general respect he inspired.

Such sentiments are scarcely compatible with the charges of impiety leveled against the Hellenists. What is more, this patriarch of the synagogue, very old at the time of the apostles, had been dead a long time when the school of Alexandria was founded. Finally, since the house of Gamaliel was an exception, the fact, whatever it was, should have disappeared with the cause—and we really do not find the least trace of it later. Offsetting this obscure and uncertain text, we find another which is in perfect accord with the strict terms of the Mishna.

> Ben Domah asked his uncle, Rabbi Ismael, for permission to study Greek science. The teacher cited the following verse to him: 'The book of the Law shall not depart out of thy mouth; thou shalt meditate on it day and night.' 'Now then,' he added, 'find an hour which is neither day nor night, and I shall permit you to devote it to the study of Greek science.'

The hypothesis that the Alexandrian philosophy found disciples among the teachers of Judea is completely demolished by the evidence of the cited passage (and we do not know of any other), which entitles us to believe that they did not even know the word "philosophy."

Indeed, what kind of philosopher was that old man who advised Hyrcanus to use the urgent requirements of their religions, which was also his own, against the enemy! Such a policy would be worthy rather of a Machiavelli! How can philosophy be counted among the attainments necessary for admission to the court of Herod! When we consult the oldest and most celebrated commentator on the Bible, R. Solomon bar Isaac, our opinion is confirmed. "By Greek science," he says, "the Talmud means a scholarly language spoken by the courtiers and not understood by the people in general." This explanation, although very sensible, is perhaps a little narrow; but, to be sure, the uncertain phrase to which it refers can only point to a certain general culture, and even more, a certain intellectual liberty brought about by the influence of Greek literature.

Where the religious traditions of the Jews show so much hatred toward all learning coming from the Greeks, is is evident from the following passage with what enthusiasm, adoration and superstitious fear they speak of the Kabbalah:

> Our teacher Yohanan ben Zakkai once took to the road, mounted on an ass and accompanied by Rabbi Eleazar ben Arak. The latter asked ben Zakkai to teach him a chapter of the Merkaba. 'Did I not tell you,' answered our teacher, 'that it is forbidden to expound the Merkaba even to one person unless he be wise and can deduce wisdom of his own accord?'
>
> 'Then permit me at least,' replied Eleazar, 'to repeat in your presence what you taught me of this science.' 'Very well, speak,' replied our teacher. And thus saying, he alighted from the ass, covered his head and sat on a stone in the shade of an olive tree. . . . Eleazar, son of Arak, had hardly begun to speak of the Merkaba, when a fire descended from heaven and enveloped all the trees of the field, which seemed to be singing hymns, and from the fire was heard the voice of an angel expressing his joy at hearing these secrets . . .

Later, when two other teachers attempted to imitate the example of Eleazar, they were struck by miracles no less astonishing. Dark clouds suddenly covered the sky, a rainbow-like meteor flashed over the horizon, and the angels were seen hastening to listen, like a curious crowd gathering to witness a wedding march.

Is it still possible to think, after reading these lines,

that the Kabbalah is but a ray pilfered from the sun of Alexandrian philosophy?

However, we must acknowledge certain resemblances between the Kabbalah and the Neo-Platonism of Alexandria, which are impossible to explain except by a common origin; for this origin, we may have to look elsewhere than in Judea and Greece. We need not point out here that the school of Ammonius, like that of Simeon ben Yohai, also shrouded itself in mystery and had resolved never to divulge the secrets of its doctrines; that, at least through the agency of their latest disciples, they too claimed to be the heirs of an ancient and mysterious tradition which, of course, emanated from a divine source; that they too were masters—and to the same degree—of the science and custom of allegorical interpretations; and, finally, that they put the alleged enlightenment of enthusiasm and faith above reason. These, then, are the claims common to all species of mysticism. We shall not dwell upon the claims but will move on to the following, more important, points:

1. To Plotinus and his disciples, as well as to the adepts of the Kabbalah, God is the immanent cause of the essential origin of things. Everything comes from Him, and everything returns to Him. He is the beginning and the end of all that is. He is, as Porphyrius says, everywhere and nowhere. He is everywhere, because all beings are in Him and through Him; He is nowhere, for He is neither in any particular existence nor in the sum of all existences. He is so far from being the union of all individual existences that he is even above existence, in which Plotinus sees but one of His manifestations. If He is superior to existence, He is equally superior to intelligence which, emanating necessarily from Him, cannot

reach Him. Then again, although He is generally called the Unity, or the First, it would be more appropriate to give Him no name at all, for there is no name that can express His essence; He is the Ineffable, the Unknown. This is exactly the status of the Ayn Sof, which the *Zohar* always calls the Unknown of Unknowns, the Mystery of Mysteries, and which it sets far above the Sefiroth, even above those which represent existence in the highest degree of abstraction.

2. According to the Alexandrian Platonists, God can be conceived only in the form of a trinity. There is, first, a general trinity composed of three terms borrowed from the language of Plato: Unity or the Good, Intelligence, and the soul of the world or the Demiurge. But each of these three expressions gives birth to a particular trinity. The Good, or Unity, in its relations to beings, is at the same time the principle of all love or the object of universal desire, the fullness of power and possession, and finally the highest perfection. As the possessor of fullness of power, God tends to manifest Himself outwardly, to become the creating cause; as the object of love and desire, He attracts to Him all that is and becomes the final cause; and as the type of highest perfection, He changes these arrangements into an efficient virtue, the beginning and end of all existence. This first trinity is called goodness itself. Next follows the intelligible trinity or divine wisdom, in whose bosom rest and unite, in most perfect identity, existence, truth and intelligible truth, that is to say, the thing that is thinking, the thing that is thought of and the thought itself. Finally, the soul of the world or the Demiurge may also be considered a trinity—the demiurgic trinity. It includes the universal substance or power which acts in all nature, the motion or generation

of beings, and their return to the bosom of the substance that produced them.

These three aspects of nature may be replaced by three others, which symbolically represent as many Olympic deities: Jupiter is the universal Demiurge of souls and bodies; Neptune reigns over the souls; and Pluto, over the bodies. These three particular trinities, which blend and lose themselves in some way in a general trinity, do not differ much from the classification of the divine attributes as represented in the *Zohar*. For we must not forget that all the Sefiroth are divided into three categories which in their totality also form a general and indivisible trinity. The first three are purely intellectual, the next three are moral, and the last relate to God as beheld in nature.

3. In the same manner, the generation of beings, or the manifestation of God's attributes, is shown by the two systems we are comparing. As stated, the doctrine of Plotinus and Proclus teaches that intelligence is the very essence of being, and that being and intelligence are absolutely identical in the bosom of unity. It follows that all existences of which the world is composed and all the aspects under which we may consider them are but a development of absolute thought or a kind of a creative dialect which simultaneously produces light, reality and life. Indeed, nothing ever divorces itself entirely from the principle or the supreme unity which is always immutable and unique; it includes all the distinguishable beings and forces in the world. In the second unity or, properly speaking, in the intelligence, thought is divided, becoming subject, object and the act of thought.

Finally, in the lower ranks, multiplicity and number are infinitely extended; while the intelligible essence of things gradually decreases until it is nothing but pure negation. In this state it becomes matter, which Porphyrius in one passage called "the absence of all existence" or a true Non-Being. The same idea is more poetically represented by Plotinus as the image of shadows which limit our knowledge and to which our soul's reflection gives intelligible form. Let us recall two remarkable passages in the *Zohar,* where thought, united at first with being in perfect identity, successively produces all creatures and divine attributes while gaining ever more varied and distinct self-awareness. The elements themselves—I mean the material elements and the various points that are to be observed in space—are among the things which it eternally produces from its own bosom. All the metaphors, therefore, which represent the supreme principle of things as a source of light inexhaustibly and eternally discharging rays that reveal its presence at all points of infinity—all these metaphors are not always to be taken literally, whether encountered in the Hebrew or the Alexandrian doctrine. Light, says Proclus expressly, is intelligence or the participation of divine intelligence. The inexhaustible source from which it flows unceasingly is absolute unity, uniting being and thought.

It would be useless to repeat about the Neo-Platonic school what has been said in our analysis of the *Zohar* about the human soul and its union with God through faith and love. All mystic systems necessarily agree on this point, for it may be regarded as the basis, the very foundation of mysticism. Can such profound and continuous resemblances in a system of ideas which is virtually inaccessible to most intelligences be explained by the sameness of human faculties or the general laws of thought? On the other hand, we believe we have sufficiently demonstrated that the teachers of Palestine could not have drawn from Greek civilization, so accursed and so anathematized by them, a science which is even more important than the study of the Law. With due regard for criticism, we cannot even conceive that the Greek philosophers could have made profitable use of the Jewish tradition. For, if Numenius and Longinus speak of Moses, and the author of *Egyptian Mysteries,* whoever he may have been, admits angels and archangels into his theological system, it is probably an effect of the translation of the Septuagint, or of the relationship between these three philosophers and the Hellenistic Jews of Egypt. It would be absurd to draw the conclusion that they were initiated in the formidable mysteries of the Merkaba.

Could there have existed an older doctrine, from which, unknown to each other, both the kabbalistic system and so-called Alexandrian Platonism sprang? There is no need to leave the capital of the Ptolemies to discover the answer. In the very midst of the Jewish nation, we find a man who is generally looked upon by historians of philosophy as the true founder of the Alexandrian school, while some critics and most modern historians of Judaism consider him the inventor of Jewish mysticism. This man is Philo. It is his system, as far as there may be one, that we shall now make the object of our investigation, endeavoring to discover in his opinions and numerous writings the first traces of the Kabbalah. I speak only of the Kabbalah, for the relations of Philo to the pagan philosophical schools which were founded after him will become apparent. Besides, no matter how worthy of interest the origin of this philosophy may be, in the present work it need be but of secondary consideration.

CHAPTER ELEVEN

The Kabbalah and the Doctrine of Philo

WITHOUT repeating what has already been said about the ignorance and isolation from each other of the Jews of Palestine and Egypt, we may add that Philo's name is never mentioned by the Jewish writers of the Middle Ages. Neither Saadia nor Maimonides, neither their later disciples nor their modern Kabbalists, have paid him any tribute, and even now he is barely known among those of his coreligionists who are strangers to Greek literature. We shall not linger upon these external facts, the importance of which we do not wish to exaggerate, but rather shall look for the solution of our problem in a philosopher's own opinions, which have been illumined by the labors of modern criticism.

There is nothing in the writings of Philo that can possibly be called a system. Incongruous opinions in disorderly juxtaposition—I refer to the symbolic interpretation of the Holy Scriptures—serve a most arbitrary method. The elements of this chaos, linked only by their common usefulness to the author in demonstrating that the Hebrew writings contain all that is most noble and most perfect in the wisdom of other nations, may be divided into two large classes. The first contains material borrowed from those Greek philosophical systems which can be reconciled with the fundamental principles of all morality and religion—like those of Pythagoras, Aristotle, Zeno and, above all, Plato, whose language and ideas were on the first plane, so to speak, in all the writings of the Hebrew philosopher. The data in the second category visibly betray their foreign origin, by their contempt for reason and science, by the impatience with which they somehow or other push the human soul headlong into infinity; this material can have only come from the Orient. This dualism in Philo's ideas is of the greatest importance, not only for the problem we are to solve, but for the history of philosophy in general.

When Philo speaks of the Creation and the first principles of existence, of God and His relations to the universe, he evidently has two doctrines in mind, which no effort of logic can ever reconcile. One doctrine is simply Plato's dualism, as taught in Timaeus; the other reminds us at the same time of Plotinus and the Kabbalah. We shall take up the first doctrine, which, oddly enough, comes from the mouth of Moses:

> The legislator of the Hebrews [says our author in his treatise on the Creation] recognized two equally necessary principles, one active and the other passive. The first is the supreme and absolute Intelligence which is above virtue, knowledge, good and beauty itself; the second is inert and inanimate matter, which became perfect when it was given movement, form and life by Intelligence.

To avoid treatment of this last principle as a pure abstraction, Philo is careful to repeat in another work the famous maxim of pagan antiquity that there is neither absolute beginning nor absolute annihilation, but that the same elements pass from one form to another. These elements are earth, water, air and fire. In order to make the world a work fully fashioned and worthy of the Supreme Architect, says Timaeus, God let no particle outside of the world. But before giving form to matter and existence in this sensual universe, God visualized in His mind the intelligible universe or the prototypes, the incorruptible ideas of things. Divine kindness, which is the sole cause for the formation of the world, also explains why the world need not perish. God cannot, without ceasing to be good, wish order and general harmony to be replaced with chaos; and to imagine that a better world must some day replace ours is to accuse God of having failed in His goodness towards the present order of things. According to this system, the generation of beings, or the application of power which formed the universe, must have necessarily commenced, but it cannot continue without end, for God cannot destroy the world, once formed, to produce another; matter cannot be returned to general chaos. Moreover, God is not the immanent cause of beings, nor the creative cause in the modern theological sense. He is only the Supreme Architect—the Demiurge—and this, in fact, is the term Philo habitually uses when he is under the influence of Greek philosophy. Finally, God is not only above, but completely outside of Creation; for he who possesses infinite knowledge and felicity cannot relate to a formless and impure substance like matter.

Let us now try to reconcile these principles with the following doctrines: God never rests in His works, but it is His nature always to produce, just as it is the nature of fire to burn and of snow to scatter cold. Rest, as applied to God, does not mean inactivity; for the active cause of the universe can never cease to produce the most beautiful works. But we say that God rests, because His infinite activity is spontaneously exerted, without pain or fatigue, so it is absurd to accept the Scriptures literally when they tell us that the world was created in six days. Far from lasting but six days, Creation did not even commence in *time*. For, according to Plato, time itself was created with other things and is but a fleeting image of eternity. Divine action, now as before, consists only of giving form to inert matter, of forcing out of disorder and darkness all the elements necessary for the formation of the world. In so doing, it becomes really creative and absolute and is no more limited in space than in duration.

"In originating things," says Philo explicitly, "God not only rendered them visible but produced what did not exist before. He is not only the Architect [the Demiurge] of the universe, He is also its Creator." He is the principle of all action in each particular being, as well as in the totality of things, for activity belongs only to Him and it is in the nature of all engendered things to be passive. It is probably because of this that everything is filled and penetrated by His presence; for the same reason He permits nothing to remain void of His presence. But since nothing can enclose the Infinite, He is nowhere and everywhere at the same time—the same antithesis we have heard from Porphyrius, understood in the same sense as it was later understood by the disciples of Plotinus. God is nowhere because place and space were created with bodies, and we cannot say that the Creator is confined in His creature. He is everywhere because He penetrates simultaneously, by His various potencies, earth and water, air and heaven. He fills the least particle of the universe, uniting each to each by invisible bonds.

This, however, is not good enough; God is Himself the universal site, for it is He Who embraces all things, Who is the shelter of the universe and His own place, wherein He confines and contains Himself. If Malebranche, who saw God only as the site of spirits, seems to be so close to Spinoza, what are we to think of one who represents the Supreme Being as the site of all existences, of spirits as well as bodies? But we must also ask what becomes of this idea of the passive principle of the universe? How are we to conceive as a real and necessary being this matter which itself has neither form nor activity, which must have existed before space—that is to say, before it was extended—and which, together with space, was transported into the bosom of God? Philo is irresistibly led to pronounce the great words: *God is All.*

How did the Supreme Being cause an actual space containing this material and sensual world to spring forth from this intelligible site which is His own substance? How did He, who is all activity and intelligence, produce passive and inactive beings? At this point the vestiges of Greek philosophy are entirely stifled by the language and ideas of the Orient. God is the purest light, the prototype and source of all light. He sheds innumerable rays of light, all intelligible, which no creature can behold, but His image is reflected in His thought (in His Logos), and it is by this image alone that we can comprehend Him. Here we see a first manifestation or, in the usual phrase, a first emanation of Divine Nature. For, when the Platonic influence yields to other influences, the divine word becomes a real being to Philo—a person or a hypostasis, as it was later called in the Alexandrian school. Such is the nature of the archangel who commands all the celestial armies.

But our philosopher does not stop at this point. From this first Logos, ordinarily called "the most ancient," the first-born of God, which represents Thought in the absolute sphere, there emanates another Logos, representing the World—that is to say, the creative power, whose manifestation is the world:

> When we read in Genesis that a river went forth from Eden to water the garden, it means that generic goodness is an emanation of Divine Wisdom, which is the Word of God. The Author of this universe should be called the Architect as well as the Father of His work. We shall give the name of Mother to Supreme Wisdom. It is with her that God united in a mysterious manner to bring about the generation of things. Impregnated with the divine seed, it is she who gave birth in pain, at the appointed time, to the well-beloved only son whom we call the world. Hence, a sacred writer represents Wisdom as saying: 'Of all the works of God, I was the first to be formed; time was not yet when I already existed. For everything that is engendered must naturally be younger than the mother and nurse of the universe.'

There is a passage in Timaeus where we find almost the same language, except for one enormous difference: the mother and nurse of all things is a principle entirely apart from God—inert and formless matter. The quoted passages are more reminiscent of the ideas and typical expressions of the *Zohar*. There, too, God is called the eternal light, and the generation of things is metaphorically explained by the gradual obfuscation of the rays emanating from the divine center and by the union of God with Himself in His diverse attributes. Supreme Wisdom, springing from the bosom of God to give life to the universe, is similarly represented by the river which goes forth from the earthly paradise. Finally, the two logoi bring to mind the kabbalistic principle that the world is but the word of God; that His word or voice is His thought become visible; and that His thought is Himself. Another image, often drawn in the principal monuments of the Kabbalah, shows the universe as a cloak or garment of God. And here it is again in the words of Philo: "The Supreme Being is surrounded by a dazzling light which envelops Him like a rich cloak, and the most ancient word covers itself with the world as with a garment."

Two ways of speaking of God result from this twofold theory on the nature and birth of things in general, when He is considered in Himself, in His own essence and independently of the Creation. Sometimes He is the supreme reason of things, the active and efficient cause of the universe, the most universal concept, the intelligible nature. He alone possesses liberty, knowledge, joy, peace and happiness—in short, perfection. Sometimes He is represented as superior to perfection itself and all possible attributes. Nothing can give us an idea of Him; neither virtue nor knowledge, nor beauty, nor goodness—not even unity. For what we call unity is but an image of the Supreme Being. All that we know of Him is that He exists; to us He is the ineffable and nameless Being.

It is easy to recognize in the first way of speaking the influence of Plato, the metaphysics of Aristotle, and even the natural philosophy of the Stoics. In the second, it is an entirely different system of ideas which reveals no less clearly the Neo-Platonic unity and the Kabbalah's Ayn Sof, the Mystery of Mysteries, the Unknown of Unknowns, which dominates both the Sefiroth and the world. The same comment, which holds for everything that Philo by virtue of his religious beliefs or philosophic views represents as an intermediary between created things and the purest essence of God, is true of the angels, the Word, and those things Philo designates under the somewhat vague name of Divine Powers. When Greek dualism is taken seriously, when the intelligent principle acts directly upon matter and God is conceived as the Demiurge of the world, the Word or the Logos becomes the divine idea, the seat of all ideas on which all beings have been patterned. The forces of messengers of God—that is, the angels at all levels of the celestial hierarchy—are the ideas themselves. This viewpoint is expressed in the following fragments:

> To speak prosaically, the intelligible world is nothing but the thought of God as He prepared to create the world, like an architect who has the ideal city in mind before he constructs a real city according to plan. Now, just as the ideal city occupies no space and is but a picture in the mind of the architect, so the intelligible world can be nothing but divine thought in which the plan for the material universe was conceived. There is no other place capable of receiving and encompassing

> even a single one of these unadulterated powers, much less all the powers of the supreme intelligence. These are the forces which have formed the immaterial and intelligible world, the prototype of the visible and corporeal world.

Elsewhere we are told that divine powers and ideas are one and the same; that their task is to give the appropriate form to each object. The angels are referred to in almost the same manner. They represent different particular forms of eternal reason or virtue, and inhabit divine space —that is to say, the intelligible world. The power upon which they directly depend, or the archangel, is, as we already know, the Logos itself. But these dispositions and roles were completely altered when God appeared in our author's mind as the immanent cause and true site of all beings. In this case, we are no longer dealing with the simple imprint of different forms upon a matter that does not exist in its own essence. Without losing an iota of their intelligible value, all ideas, moreover, become substantial realities, active forces, subordinated to one another and yet bound in one substance, one force, one single intelligence.

Wisdom, or the Word, thus becomes the first of all heavenly influences, a distinct power, but not separate from the Absolute Being, the spring that waters and vitalizes the earth, the cup-bearer of the Almighty, who pours the nectar of the souls and is himself this nectar, the first-born of God, and the mother of all beings. He is also called divine man, for the image in which earthly man was created on the sixth day and which the Holy Scriptures call the image of God is the eternal Word. It is the high priest of the universe—that is to say, the conciliator between the finite and the infinite. It may be regarded as a second God without impairing belief in one God. This is what is meant in the Scriptures whenever titles and a name are bestowed upon God; for the first rank belongs to the ineffable being. Philo's assertion that the Word sometimes reveals itself to man in material form fully convinces us that these expressions refer to a real personification. It is the Word that the patriarch Jacob saw in a dream, and it is the Word again that spoke to Moses out of the burning bush.

We have already seen how this supreme Word engenders another, which emanates from it like a river gushing from its source. This second word is goodness, creative virtue, a hypostatized Platonic idea. Below goodness is royal power, which justly governs all created beings. The latter two forces are called Mercy and Justice, when their practices are confined to men. All three forces revealed themselves once upon the earth in the guise of the three angels who visited Abraham. They make up the invisible good and harmony of this world, just as they are the glory, the presence of God, whence they descend by a gradual darkening of the infinite splendor. For each one of them is both shadow and light; shadow of that which is above, light and life of all that is below their own sphere.

Their essence, finally, is just as impossible to comprehend as that of the primitive being, although their action is present everywhere and their forms manifest themselves in those of the universe. It is what God Himself taught Moses, says Philo, when the latter implored Him to show him at least His glory—that is to say, the forces that surround His inaccessible throne—after asking in vain to see Him face to face. The angels, described as ideas representing different kinds of virtue, are not only personified after the manner of poets and biblical writers; they are also looked upon as souls floating in ether, sometimes uniting with souls inhabiting human bodies. They form real and animated substances which impart life to all elements and all parts of nature:

> The beings which philosophers of other nations call demons are called angels by Moses. These are the souls that float in the air, and no one must deny their existence; for the universe must be animated in all its parts, and each element must be inhabited by living beings. The earth is thus stocked with animals, the sea and rivers with the inhabitants of water, fire with the salamander—supposedly quite common in Macedonia—the heavens with stars. In fact, if the stars were not pure and divine souls, they would not be endowed with circular motion, which properly belongs to the spirit only. It follows that the air must also be peopled by living beings, although our eyes cannot see them.

Philo's syncretism and the twofold direction to which he commits himself, notwithstanding his lively predilection for Oriental ideas, are most easily seen when he deals with man. Thus, unlike Plato, he is not content with seeing the pale imprint of eternal ideas in material things; but he goes on to maintain that without the help of the senses we can never rise to higher cognition, that without the spectacle of the material world we cannot even suspect the existence of an immaterial and invisible world. He then declares the influence of the senses to be absolutely harmful and commands man to sever all connections with them and to take refuge within himself. He creates an abyss between the rational, intelligent soul, which alone is privileged to constitute man, and the sentient soul, from which our organs borrow life as well as the knowledge appropriate to them. This soul resides, as Moses said, in the blood, while the other is an emanation, an inseparable reflection of divine nature.

This exalted point of view does not prevent Philo from retaining the Platonic view of the human soul which recognizes three elements: thought, will and passions. In innumerable places he insists upon the necessity of preparing for wisdom by what he calls "encyclical sciences"—that is to say, by oratory and those skills which contribute to the external culture so dear to the Greeks. Our mind, he says, must be nourished with such mundane knowledge before it can aspire to higher science, just as our body must be nourished with milk before it can assimilate more substantial food. He who neglects to acquire this knowledge must succumb in this world as Abel succumbed to the blows of his fratricidal brother.

In another place he teaches entirely the contrary: The word and outward appearance are to be scorned, just as the body and senses are, that we may live in intelligence and the contemplation of the naked truth alone. God's command to Abraham to leave his country, his family and his father's house means that man must break away from his body, his senses and the word. For the body is but part of the earth where we are forced to live; the senses are the servants and brothers of thought; and the word, finally, is but the cover and in some measure the dwelling place of intelligence, which is our real father.

The same thought is symbolically reproduced in a more expressive way by Hagar and Ishmael. This rebellious servant and her son, so ignominiously driven from their master's house, represent encyclical knowledge and the sophism it begets. It is hardly necessary to add that he who aspires to a higher level of the spiritual world must imitate the Hebrew patriarch. But when the soul takes refuge in intelligence, does it at least find there the means to fulfill itself and through itself to arrive at truth and wisdom? Had Philo answered this question in the affirmative, he would have gone beyond the doctrine of Plato. To Plato, only he is truly wise who entirely renounces body and senses and labors all his life to learn how to die. But our Alexandrian philosopher oversteps this boundary; in addition to the knowledge borrowed from reason and the enlightenment given to philosophy, man also needs enlightenment and higher knowledge emanating directly from God and communicated to intelligence as a favor, a mysterious gift.

When we read in the Scriptures, Philo says, that God spoke to man, we are not to believe that the atmosphere was shattered by a material voice but that the human soul had been illumined by the purest light. Only in this manner can the divine word address itself to man. Again, when the Law was promulgated on Mount Sinai, the text does not say that a voice was *heard,* but that a voice was *seen* by all the people assembled. "You have seen," says Jehovah, "that I spoke to you from heaven above." Since a miracle is expounded, this cannot refer to rational knowledge or to a mere contemplation of ideas, but to a revelation mystically understood. We shall give the same meaning to another passage offering the possibility of man's grasping God Himself through direct manifestation instead of rising to Him by the contemplation of His works. In this state, adds our author, we understand at a glance the essence of God, his word and the universe. Philo recognizes faith, which he calls "the queen of virtues," as the most perfect of all goodness, the cement that unites divine nature. It is faith that is represented in the story of Judah and Tamar; for as Judah united with Tamar without lifting the veil that covered her face, so does faith unite us with God.

Philo shows the same hesitation when speaking of human liberty as when explaining the nature and origin of our knowledge. At times the Stoic doctrine that man is free triumphs; the laws of necessity which govern without exception all other creatures do not exist for man. Free choice, then, which is man's privilege, imposes upon him at the same time responsibility for his actions; only thus is man alone of all beings capable of virtue, and we are justified in saying that God, wishing to manifest Himself in the universe through the idea of goodness, found no temple more dignified than the human soul. But it is early seen that this theory, so true and wise, contradicts certain general principles previously expounded; e.g., the unity of substance, the formation of being by way of emanation, and even Platonic dualism.

Nor does our philosopher scruple to abandon this theory for an opposite one—with which he obviously finds himself more at ease—revealing the wealth of his semi-Oriental style and the resources of his natural genius. Here he relieves man of free choice as well as moral responsibility. The evil we attribute to ourselves as one which generally reigns in this world is the inevitable fruit of matter or the work of inferior forces which participated with the divine Logos in the formation of man. Good, on the contrary, belongs to God alone. It is really because it does not suit the Supreme Being to participate in evil that He called for subordinate workers to cooperate with Him in the creation of Adam; all the good in our actions and thoughts must be attributed to Him alone.

According to this principle, it is boastful and impious to consider oneself the author of any work; to do so, means to compare oneself with God, Who alone deposited in our soul the germ of good, and Who alone is qualified to impregnate it. This quality, without which we would be swallowed up by evil and blended with nothingness or matter, Philo calls by its true name, Grace.

Along with this quite mystical influence, Philo admits another, which equally endangers moral responsibility and, consequently, free choice. It is the reversibility of good. The righteous is the expiatory victim of the wicked, and it is for the sake of the righteous that God lavishes upon the wicked His inexhaustible treasures. This dogma, adopted by the Kabbalists and applied by them to the entire universe, is fundamentally a development of Grace. Grace alone brings merit to the righteous; why then not to the wicked as well? As to that other obstacle to human liberty—the original sin—it would not be impossible to find its definition in some isolated words of this author. But on such an important subject we must expect more explicit and definite proofs. We can confidently assert that Philo considered life itself as a state of forfeiture and compulsion; consequently, the more man enters life, or the further he penetrates the realm of nature through will or intelligence, the further he wanders from God, becoming perverted and degraded. This principle is almost the sole basis for Philo's morality.

Despite occasional contradictions, the Greek influence extends only to the language; the background is entirely Oriental and mystic. For example, when Philo tells us, as Antisthenes and Zeno do, that we must live according to nature, he understands by human nature not only the entire domination of Spirit over body, of reason over sense, but also observance of all the revealed laws, undoubtedly as he intercepted and understood them. When, like Plato and the Stoic school, he admits what were later called the "four virtues," he represents them as inferior and purely human virtues; above these he shows us their common source of goodness or love, a purely religious virtue which concerns itself with God alone, Whose image and purest emanation it is. It springs directly from Eden, that is to say, from Divine Wisdom, where alone joy, pleasure and delight in God are found. It is probably in this sense, and following the example of Socrates, that he identifies virtue with wisdom.

We must, finally, take care not to attribute Aristotle's thoughts to Philo when, using that philosopher's terms, he says that virtue may come from three sources: knowledge, nature and exercise. True science and wisdom, according to Philo, is not that which results from a natural development of our intelligence, but is given to us by the grace of God. According to the Greek philosopher, nature itself impels us toward good; according to Philo, there are in man two entirely opposite and conflicting natures, one of which must necessarily succumb; following this, both are in a state of violence and restraint which permit them no rest. Whence his third expedient to attain moral perfection: substitution of the most exalted asceticism for the lawful authority of will and reason over our desires. Indeed, at issue is not simply the attenuation of evil or its restriction to more or less defined limits; but evil must be pursued as long as there is the least trace of it; must be destroyed, if possible, root and branch. For the evil we suffer in this world resides entirely in our passions, which Philo considers absolutely foreign to the nature of the soul. The passions, to use his language, have their origin in the flesh. The flesh, therefore, must be humiliated and mortified; it must be combated in every way and in all instances; we must raise ourselves from this state of forfeiture called life; we must regain liberty in the very bosom of that prison which we call the body by absolute indifference to all perishable possessions.

Since the purpose and result of marriage is the perpetuation of this state of misery, Philo, without openly condemning it, looks upon marriage as a humiliating necessity from which select souls ought to liberate themselves.

These, by and large, are the principal characteristics of the ascetic life, more as Philo conceived them than as he had seen them practiced by the Therapeutic sect. But the ascetic life is only a means; the aim of morality, itself the highest degree of perfection, happiness and existence, is the union of the soul with God through total forgetfulness of itself, through enthusiasm and through love.

Here are some passages which sound as though they have been borrowed from some modern mystic:

> O, my soul! If you desire to inherit heavenly gifts, it is not only necessary, as our first patriarch did, to abandon the land you inhabit, that is to say, your body; the family you were born in, that is to say, the senses; and the house of your father, or the word; you must also abandon yourself that you may be outside of yourself like those Corybants who are intoxicated with divine enthusiasm.

The contemplative life—although it may not be the only one—is placed by such principles far above all social virtues whose principle is love and whose aim is the well-being of man. Not even the cult—I mean the external cult—can lead us to our goal. Philo is really very confused on this point.

> Just as we must take care of the body, since it is the dwelling place of the soul, so must we observe the written laws; for the truer we are to them, the better will we understand the things they symbolize. In addition to this we must avoid blame and accusations from the multitude.

The last remark sounds very much like a postscript. It alone expresses the philosopher's thinking and establishes a closer relationship between him and the Kabbalists. It also justifies the opinion the Talmudists had of their brethren who were initiated in Greek learning.

Two extremely important conclusions can be drawn from all of the foregoing regarding the origin of the Kabbalah. The first is that this traditional doctrine was not derived from the writings of Philo. Indeed, since all Greek systems—in fact, the entire Greek civilization—have left so many traces in his writings, why are they not similarly to be found in the oldest writings of the kabbalistic science? We reiterate: nowhere—either in the *Zohar* or the Book of Formation—is there to be found the least trace of that splendid civilization which was transplanted by the Ptolemies to Egyptian soil. Is it possible that Simeon ben Yohai and his friends, or whoever the authors of the *Zohar* may have been, could have distinguished—with nothing but Philo's writing to guide them—between that which had been borrowed from various Greek philosophers, whose names are seldom mentioned by their Alexandrian disciples, and that which belonged to another doctrine based upon the idea of one immanent principle which is the substance and form of all beings? Such a supposition is unworthy of discussion.

Besides, what we have called the Oriental aspect of Philo's syncretism is far from corresponding in all important points with the mysticism taught by the Palestinian sages. Thus, according to Philo, there are only five divine forces or attributes, while the Kabbalists admit ten Sefiroth. Even when he enthusiastically expounds the doctrine of emanation and absolute unity, Philo always preserves a certain dualism—the Absolute Being and forces or the substance and attributes, separated by an unbridgeable gulf. The Kabbalists look upon the Sefiroth as diverse boundaries within which the absolute principle of things circumscribes itself—or as "vessels," to use their language. The divine substance, they add, need only withdraw, and these vessels would break and spill over. Let us also remember that they expressly taught the identity of existence and thought. Philo, who is unconsciously dominated by the idea (of Plato and Anaxagoras) that matter is a principle distinct from God and as everlasting as He, is naturally led to consider life a forfeiture and the body a prison.

This also accounts for his contempt for marriage, which he regards merely as a gratification of the flesh. The Kabbalists, on the other hand, although agreeing with Scriptures that in the first days of the Creation when man was not ruled by sensual passions he was happier than now, still look upon life in general as a necessary trial, as a means through which finite beings may elevate themselves to God and unite with Him in boundless love. To them, marriage is not only the symbol, but the beginning, the first condition of this mysterious union; they introduce marriage into the soul and into heaven. It is the fusion of two human souls by mutual completion. Finally, the system of interpretation which Philo applies to the Holy Scriptures, although basically identical with that of the Kabbalists, could not have served as their pattern.

Philo was surely not entirely ignorant of the language of his fathers; but we can easily prove that he had only the Septuagint version before him, the version of the Bible used by all the Alexandrian Jews. His mystic interpretations are based mainly on the diction of this translation and a purely Greek etymology. Then what is to become of those ingenious procedures used in the *Zohar*, whose force is entirely destroyed if not applied to the sacred language? Moreover, we acknowledge that this difference in form would be less important to us if Philo and the Kabbalists were always in accord on their scriptural passages or, indeed, if language aside, the same symbols kindled the same ideas. But this is never so. Thus we do not find either in the *Zohar* or the Book of Formation the least trace of those rich and ingenious allegories which we consider the sole property of the Alexandrian philosopher. No mention is made of the personification of the senses in woman, in Eve, our first mother; of voluptuousness in the serpent which counseled evil; of Cain's egotism, evoked by Adam's union with Eve, that is to say, with the senses, when he heeded the serpent; of Abel, the spiritual type, who wholly despises the body and succumbs through ignorance of mundane things; of Abraham, symbol of divine knowledge; of Haggar's worldly knowledge; of Sarah's virtue; of the primitive nature of regenerated man in Isaac; or ascetic virtue in Jacob and of faith in Tamar. For these reasons, we believe we have the right to say that Philo's writings exerted no influence whatever upon the Kabbalah.

We come now to the second conclusion which may be drawn from these writings and from the character of their author. We have seen how indiscriminately and with what disregard for sound logic Philo pillaged, so to speak, the entire Greek philosophy. Why then should we credit him with greater inventiveness, sagacity and profundity in those of his views which recall the dominant principles of the kabbalistic system? Is it not legitimate to think that he found this material, ready made, in some of the traditions of his coreligionists, and that he only embellished it with the brilliant colors of his imagination? These traditions were quite old: for Egypt must have received them from the Holy Land before the memory of Jerusalem and the language of their fathers were entirely extinguished among the Alexandrian Jews.

Fortunately, we need not rely upon conjecture. There are facts which prove conclusively that some of the ideas under discussion were known more than a century before the Christian era. First, Philo himself assures us that he drew upon an oral tradition preserved by the elders of his people, attributing to the Therapeutic sect the mystic books of a very remote antiquity (*De Vita contemplativa*) and the use of allegorical interpretation as applied without exception and without reserve to all parts of the Holy Scriptures. "The entire law," he says, "is to them like a living being in which the body is represented by letters and the soul by a very deep meaning. Through words, as through a mirror, the rational soul perceives the most hidden and extraordinary wonders." Let us keep in mind that the same comparison is used in the *Zohar*, with the difference that above the body is the vestment of the Law, to indicate the material facts of the Bible; above the soul is a holier soul—that is to say, the Divine Word—source of all inspiration and truth. But we have testimony still older and more reliable than Philo's. We shall begin with the most important of all, the famous version of the Septuagint.

The Talmud was vaguely aware of the numerous inaccuracies in this famous translation, which it nevertheless venerated profoundly. Modern criticism has conclusively proven that the translation was made in behalf of a system eminently hostile to biblical anthropomorphism, and in which is to be found the germ of Philo's mysticism. Thus, when the sacred text (Exod. 24: 9,10) expressly states that Moses, his brother and the seventy elders saw the God of Israel setting upon a sapphire stone, the Greek translation says that is not God they saw, but His dwelling place. When another prophet, Isaiah, sees God sitting upon His throne, the folds of His robe filling the temple (Isa. 6: 1), this image, too material for the Septuagint, is replaced with the "glory of God," the Shekinah of the Hebrews. Jehovah does not really speak to Moses face to face, but in a vision; and it is probable that in the mind of the translator this vision was purely intellectual.

Until this point we have seen only the destruction of anthropomorphism and the desire to disengage the idea of God from the sometimes sublime images which put Him beyond our intelligence. But now matters become more interesting. Instead of Lord Zebaot, God of Hosts, whom the Bible represents as another Mars exciting the fury of war and himself marching into battle—(The Lord will go forth as a mighty man, He will stir up jealousy like a man of war—Isa. 42: 13)—we find in the Greek translation not the Supreme God, but the forces of which Philo speaks so much in his writings: The Lord, God of Powers. When comparison is made to the "dew born of the womb of dawn"—(From the womb of the dawn, thine is the dew of thy youth—Ps. 110: 3)—the anonymous translator substitutes for the mysterious being which God brought forth from his bosom before dawn, the morning star—that is to say, the Logos, the divine light which preceded the world and the stars.

In this curious and monumental translation, we also find unquestionable traces of the theory of numbers and ideas. For example: God is not the creator of heaven and earth in the ordinary sense of the word; He simply made them visible from the invisible state they were previously in (Isa. 45:18). "Who created all these?" asks the Hebrew prophet. "Who created them visible?" (Isa. 40:26), says the Alexandrian interpreter. When the same prophet represents the Master of the Universe as commanding the stars like a numerous army, our interpreter has him declare that God produced the world by number. While an allusion to the doctrines of Plato and Pythagoras is easily found in these diverse passages, we must not forget that the theory of numbers is also taught, although in a rough way, in the *Sefer Yetzirah,* and that the theory of ideas is absolutely inseparable from the metaphysics of the *Zohar.*

We must note that an application of the Pythagorean principle found in the *Sefer Yetzirah* is literally reproduced in the writings of Philo and would be vainly sought in the works of any other philosopher writing in Greek. It holds that it is due to the influence of the number seven that we possess seven principal organs: the five senses, the organ of speech, and the generative organs; and for the same reason there are seven gates of the soul, to wit: two eyes, two ears, two nostrils, and one mouth. The Septuagint also has another kabbalistic tradition which was later appropriated by gnosticism. Although the Bible says that "the Most High set the borders of the nations according to the number of children of Israel," we read in the Alexandrian translation that "the nations were divided according to the number of the Lord's angels." (Deut. 32:8.) This apparently odd and arbitrary interpretation becomes intelligible when compared with a passage in the *Zohar* where we learn that there are seventy nations on earth and that each of these nations is under the domination of an angel whom it recognizes as its God, and who, so to speak, is the personification of its own spirit. The children of Israel alone are privileged to have over them none but the true God Who has chosen them as His people. We find the same tradition in a sacred writer no less ancient than the Septuagint, Jesus ben Sirach.

No doubt, the Greek philosophy, which flourished in the capital of the Ptolemies, exercised a great influence upon this famous translation. But we find ideas in the Septuagint which have evidently been drawn from another source and which could not even have been brought forth upon Egyptian soil. For were it otherwise—that is, if all the elements we have noted such as the allegoric interpretation of the religious elements, the personification of the Word and its identity with the absolute place—if these were part of the general trend of Egyptian thought in that period, how is it that over a period of two centuries, from the time of the last authors of the Septuagint version of Philo, there is not the least mention of that trend in the history of Greek philosophy? But we have another, nearly contemporaneous record wherein we find the same spirit in a more definite form, the Hebrew origin of which cannot be contested. It is the book of Jesus, son of Sirach, commonly called Ecclesiasticus.

This religious author is known to us at present only through Greek translation by his grandson, who tells us in a sort of preface that he came to Egypt (probably after leaving Judea) in the thirty-eighth year of the reign of

Evergetes II. Assuming that the original writer lived fifty years earlier, that would place him two centuries before the Christian era. Without imparting implicit faith to the testimony of the translator, who assures us that his grandfather drew only upon the Hebrew, let us note that Jesus, son of Sirach, is often eulogized by the Talmud under the name of Joshua ben Sirach ben Eliezer. The original text still existed at the time of St. Jerome, and as late as the beginning of the fourth century Jews as well as Gentiles counted it among their sacred writings. We find in the writings of this ancient author not only the traditions which we have discussed but also the doctrine of the Logos or Divine Wisdom, in nearly the same form as taught by Philo and the Kabbalists.

Wisdom is, first of all, the same power as the Word, or the *Memra* of the Chaldean translators. It is *the* Word; it issued from the mouth of the Most High; it cannot be taken as a simple abstraction, as a purely logical being, for it manifests itself in the midst of the people, in the assembly of the Most High, and praises its soul. This heavenly assembly is probably composed of forces subordinate to the Word; for the Talmud and *Zohar* make frequent use of a very similar expression to convey the same thought. Wisdom, thus introduced upon the scene, presents itself as the first-born of God; for it existed at the very beginning, when time was not yet, and it will not cease to exist in the course of the ages. Wisdom has always been with God; it is through wisdom that the world was created; Wisdom alone formed the celestial spheres and descended to the depths of the abyss. Its empire extends over the waves of the ocean, over all regions of the earth, and over all the peoples and all the nations that inhabit it. Having been ordered by God to look for a dwelling place on earth, Wisdom's choice fell on Zion.

When we consider that to ben Sirach every other nation is subject to the influence of an angel or a subordinate power, we must look upon the choice of Zion as the dwelling place for Wisdom as no simple metaphor. On the contrary, the choice shows, as the tradition cited expressly asserts, that the spirit of God, or the Logos, acted directly, without an intermediary, on the prophets of Israel. If Wisdom were not substantial, if it were not in some way the instrument and servant of God, how could it be conceived as sitting upon a throne within a column of clouds—the same column, probably, that marched before the Hebrew people in the desert? In sum, the spirit of this book, like the Septuagint version and the Chaldaic paraphrases of Onkelos, is based on the separation of the Sovereign Being and this perishable world by a mediating power which is at the same time eternal and the first work of God; which acts and speaks for Him; and which is itself His word and His creative power. The abyss between the finite and the infinite is thus filled; heaven and earth are no longer divorced; God manifests Himself through His word, and His word through the universe. But the Divine Word has no need of first being recognized in visible things; it sometimes comes directly to man in the form of a holy inspiration or through the gift of prophecy and revelation.

It was thus that the nation was raised above all other nations, and one man, the lawgiver of the Hebrews, above all other men. There is no conflict on this important issue between theology and criticism. For when we consult the most orthodox translations of Ecclesiasticus, Sacy's for example, we find many allusions to the doctrine of the

Word. We may say the same of the Book of Wisdom:

> Wisdom is more active than the most active thing. . . . It is the breath—that is to say, an emanation of God's power—and a very pure effusion of the brightness of the Almighty. It is the reflection of everlasting light, the spotless mirror of the majesty of God and the image of His goodness. Although only one, it can accomplish everything, and resting immutably in itself it renews all things. It enters at different times into holy souls and makes them prophets and friends of God. (Ch. 7:24-27.)

But it seems to us that the general character of this work comes nearer to the Platonic philosophy than to the mysticism of Philo. And as neither its age nor true origin are known, we must wait for a more learned critic to settle these questions. However, the facts we have collected demonstrate fully that the Kabbalah is neither the fruit of the Greek civilization of Alexandria, nor of pure Platonism. In fact, we find the principle which serves as basis of the entire Kabbalistic system, namely, the personification of the Word and of Divine Wisdom considered as the immanent cause of beings, in a period when the specific Alexandrian spirit was still in the process of being born. We find it, furthermore, in a traditional translation, so to speak, of the Scriptures and in another monument of purely Hebrew origin. When details and secondary ideas are considered, the great differences between the writings of Philo and of the Hebrew Kabbalists become evident.

CHAPTER TWELVE

The Kabbalah and Christianity

SINCE THE Kabbalah is indebted neither to philosophy nor to Greece, nor to the capital of the Ptolemies, it necessarily must have its cradle in Asia. Judaism must have brought it forth through its own efforts; or it must have sprung from some other Oriental religion so close to Judaism as to exert an unquestionable influence upon it. Is it possible that Christianity is that religion?

Notwithstanding the extreme interest aroused at first by this question, we cannot pause to consider it at any length. It is evident that all the great metaphysical and religious principles underlying the Kabbalah antedate the

Christian dogmas. It is not, however, within the scope of our work to compare them.

But no matter what meaning we may ascribe to these principles, their form alone explains to us a fact of very great social and religious interest. A great many medieval Kabbalists converted to Christianity. Among others, Paul Ricci, Conrod Otton, and Rittangel, the last editor of the *Sefer Yetzirah.* Otton was the author of *Gali Razia* (*Unveiled Secrets*), published in Nuremberg, 1605. The aim of this work, composed entirely of Hebrew quotations translated into Latin and German, was to prove the Christian dogma by reference to various passages from the Talmud and *Zohar.* In more recent times, toward the end of the eighteenth century, another Kabbalist, the Polish Jew Jacob Frank, passed into the bosom of Catholicism with several thousand of his adherents, after founding the sect of the Zoharites. The rabbinate has for a long time perceived this danger; many rabbis have evinced their hostility to the study of the Kabbalah, while others protect it even today as the holy ark, as the entrance to the Holy of Holies, to keep the profane away. Leon de Modena, whose *Ari Noham* (*The Roaring Lion*) was published in Leipzig in 1840—a book contesting the authenticity of the *Zohar*—very much doubts the salvation of those who published the principal kabbalistic works. On the other hand, Christians, like Knorr von Rosenroth, Reuchlin and Rittangel after his conversion, regarded the Kabbalah as the most potent means of lowering the barrier that separates synagogue and church. In the hope of some day bringing about this fervently desired result, they collected in their works all the passages of the *Zohar* and the New Testament which present some similarity to one another.

Let us now investigate whether there is anything in common between the Kabbalah and the most ancient organs of Gnosticism. We shall thus ascertain whether the kabbalistic principles were not widespread outside of Judea, whether they did not also influence other peoples who were complete strangers to Greek civilization, and whether accordingly, we are not justified in regarding these principles as precious remnants of a religious philosophy of the Orient. Transplanted to Alexandria, mingled with the doctrines of Plato, and under the usurped name of Dionysius the Areopagite, this philosophy penetrated the mysticism of the Middle Ages.

Without leaving Palestine, we first meet at Samaria, in the days of the apostles, and probably at an advanced age, a very singular person, Simon the Magician (Magus). Who was this man who enjoyed such incontestable power (Acts 8: 10) and boundless admiration among his fellow citizens?

It is the prevailing opinion that Simon came from Githoi, a small Samaritan town. The historian Josephus is the only one to mention a Jew, originally from Cyprus, who pretended to be a magician. Although he may have had a base enough view of the motive which prompts us to share the most sublime gifts with others, he surely was no impostor, for he looked up to the apostles and wanted to buy the prerogative to impart the holy spirit (Acts 8: 18, 19). I will go further and say that his authority would have been in vain were it not supported by a well-known and long accepted popular idea. We find this idea very clearly expressed in the supernatural role attributed to Simon. All the people, say the Acts, from the highest to the lowest, considered him the personification of the great power of God: *Hic est virtus Dei quae vocatur magna* (This man is the great power of God).

Now St. Jerome tells us that our Samaritan prophet understood this to be nothing other than the Word of God (*Sermo Dei*). Having this quality he must have necessarily united in him all the other divine attributes; for according to the religious metaphysics of the Hebrews, the Word or Wisdom implicitly includes the lower Sefiroth. St. Jerome also describes as authentic Simon's self-appraisal: "I am the Divine Word, I possess true beauty, I am the comforter, I am the Almighty, I am all that is in God." Each of these expressions correspond to one of the Sefiroth of the Kabbalah, whose influence we find again in a report by Clement, another church father: "Simon the Magician, who considered himself the visible manifestation of the Word, also wished to personify divine thought in a woman of bad repute"—that is to say, its correlative female principle or spouse.

This strange conception finds no support either in the Platonic philosophy or in the Alexandrian school—if the latter even existed by that time. But it is a distorted reflection of the kabbalistic system, where Wisdom, that is the Word represented as the male principle, has a complementary half, a wife—in this case the Sefiroth called Intelligence. Intelligence has been taken by several Gnostics for the Holy Spirit, being always represented by them in the form of a woman. These Gnostics include the Jew Elxai, who has many features of resemblance to the prophet of Samaria. Even his name—which he surely chose himself—suggests the role he assumed. This heresiarch not only conceives the Holy Spirit as a female principle, but views Christ as nothing but a divine power which sometimes assumes a physical shape whose colossal proportions he describes in minute detail.

We recall a similar description, of the White Head, in the *Zohar;* another work, very famous among the Kabbalists, the pseudonymous "Alphabet of Rabbi Akiba," speaks of God in nearly the same terms. Alongside of this kind of conception of the Word, the Holy Spirit, and in general the divine pairs of which the Pleroma is composed, the kabbalistic cosmogonic principle is also to be found in the writings of the Syrian Bardasanes. The unknown father who lives in the center of light has a son; this is Christ, or the heavenly man. Christ, in his turn, in uniting with his companion, his spouse, which is the Holy Ghost, successively produces the four elements, air, water, fire and earth. In a way, these elements and the external world in general are, as in the *Sefer Yetzirah,* a simple emanation or the voice of the spirit.

Why persist in laboriously gleaning the scattered impressions of the Acts of the Apostles or the Hymns of St. Ephrem, when we can draw quite liberally from a much more valuable work, the *Codex Nazareus*—that bible of purely Oriental Gnosticism. We know that St. Jerome and St. Epiphanius date the sect of the Nazarenes to the time of the birth of Christ. The similarity between many of their dogmas and the most essential elements of the kabbalistic system is so great as to make us believe we have found some stray fragments of the *Zohar* in the *Codex.* Thus, God is always called the King and Master of Light; He is Himself splendor—Infinite and Eternal Light. He is also beauty, life, justice and mercy. All the shapes that we perceive in this world emanate from Him; He is the creator and the architect, but no one perceives His essential wisdom and essence. All creatures ask one another for His name, and they are compelled to answer that He has none. As the king of light, infinite light, He has no name that can be invoked, no nature that can be known; we can reach Him only through a pure heart, an upright spirit and a faith replete with love. The steps by which the Nazarene doctrine descends from the highest being to the furthest limits of the Creation are exactly the same as in a passage of the *Zohar* we have frequently quoted:

> Spirits, kings and creatures vie to celebrate in prayers and hymns the supreme king of light, who sends forth five rays of marvelous brilliancy. The first is the light that illumines all beings; the second is the mild breath that animates them; the third is the melodious voice that expresses their cheerfulness; the fourth is the word which instructs them and elevates them to bear witness to their faith; the fifth is the prototype of all forms under which they develop, like fruit which ripens under the sun.

We cannot fail to recognize in these lines the different degrees of existence which the Kabbalists represent by thought, breath or spirit, voice and word. Here are other images, no less familiar, which express the same idea: Before there were any creatures, life was hidden within itself, eternal and incomprehensible, without light and without form. From which is also called the Word, the Garment, or the symbolical river that represents Wisdom. From this river flow the living waters, or the great waters which to the Nazarenes as well as the Kabbalists, represent the third manifestation of God, Intelligence or Spirit. This produces in its turn a second life, far removed from the first. This second life is called *Yushamin* and in its bosom was first conceived the idea of the Creation, of which it is the loftiest and purest type.

The second life engendered a third, which is called the "principal father," the "unknown graybeard" and "the old man of the world." When the principal father looked into the abyss, the gloom of the black waters, he left his image there, which, under the name of Fetahil, became the Demiurge or architect of the universe. Then begins an interminable series of eons, an infernal and celestial hierarchy which has no further interest for us. It is enough to know that these three lives, these three degrees which can be distinguished in the Pleroma, hold the same rank as the three kabbalistic faces, whose very designation is often found on the lips of these sectarians. This interpretation is all the more acceptable as they too, like the *Zohar,* divide the ten Sefiroth into three supreme and seven inferior attributes.

As for the singular accident which brought forth the Demiurge, and the more and more imperfect generation of the subordinate spirits, these are mythological expressions of the principle that darkness and evil are but the gradual weakening of divine light. It is also very clearly formulated in the Nazarene code. Hence the name "body" or "matter" assigned to the Prince of Darkness.

The Nazarenes also recognized two Adams, one celestial and invisible, the other earthly, the father of humanity. By virtue of his body, the earthly Adam is the work of the subordinate spirits, the stellar spirits; but his soul is an emanation of divine life. This soul, which was to return to its father in the heavenly regions, seduced by evil powers, was detained in this world. The message the Kabbalists entrusted to the angel Raziel, our heretics give to Gabriel, who plays an important role in their belief. It was he who brought the true law, the word of life, mysteriously spread by tradition until the advent of John the Baptist, to our primal parents to raise them after their fall and open the way to the bosom of their father. John the Baptist was the true prophet, according to the Nazarenes, who pronounced it on the shores of the Jordan.

Were we now to meet the same principles in Egyptian Gnoticism, in the doctrines of Basilides and Valentin, it would be unjust to attribute them to Greek philosophy, or even to Alexandrian Neo-Platonism. And, in fact, it would be very easy to demonstrate in the fragments left by these two celebrated heresiarchs, the most characteristic elements of the Kabbalah: the unity of substance, the formation of things first by concentration, then by the gradual expansion of divine light, the theory of pairs and of four worlds, the two Adams, the three souls, and even the symbolic language of numbers and the letters of the alphabet. But there is nothing to be gained from such a demonstration for we believe we have achieved the goal we set ourselves for this last part of our work. We established previously that the metaphysical ideas comprising the foundation of the Kabbalah were not borrowed from Greek philosophy but were brought to Alexandria from Palestine; now we have proven that the cradle of the Kabbalah is not to be found in Palestine, or at least in Judea.

For despite the impenetrable mystery with which the teachers of the synagogue surrounded the kabbalistic teachings, we find them, in a less abstract and pure form, it is true, in the infidel capital of the Samarians and among the heretics of Syria. It matters little that since they were here taught to be people as a religious fundamental, they were characterized by mythological personification, while in Palestine, having become the property of the intellectual elite, they constituted a great metaphysical system.

The basis of these ideas remains ever the same; nothing is changed in their interrelation—neither in the formulas with which they are invested, nor in the more or less bizarre traditions that accompany them. We have still to determine which Oriental religion served as a springboard for their direct penetration of Judaism.

CHAPTER THIRTEEN

The Kabbalah and the Religion of the Chaldeans and Persians

WERE WE to find within the circumscribed limits of our investigation a people as distinguished by their civilization as by their political power that exercised an immediate and prolonged influence upon the Hebrews, we could, it is evident, solve the problem we have raised. These conditions are fulfilled by the Chaldeans and Persians, united into one nation by the arms of Cyrus and the religion of Zoroaster. And indeed, can we think of an event in the life of a people more likely to change its moral constitution and modify its ideas and customs than the memorable exile that has been called the Babylonian Captivity? Could the seventy years' sojourn of the Israelites, priests and laymen, teachers and common people, in the land of their conquerors have exerted no influence on either side? We have already cited a talmudic passage where the elders of the synagogue openly acknowledge that their ancestors brought with them from the land of their exile the names of the angels and the months, and even the letters of the alphabet.

It must be supposed that the names of the months were accompanied by some astronomical and astrological knowledge, probably akin to what we have met in the *Sefer Yetzirah,* and that it was possible entirely to separate the names of the angels from the celestial and infernal hierarchy adopted by the Magi. It has also long since been noted that Satan's first appearance in the sacred writings is in the story of the Chaldean Job. This rich and learned mythology, which was adopted by the Talmud and is widespread in the Mishna, also constitutes the poetry and, if I may use the expression, the outer wrappings of the *Zohar*. But let us disregard the Chaldeans, who left no extensive or reliable works and who, besides, were morally and physically conquered by the Persians before the return of the Jews to the Holy Land. Instead, we shall prove the presence, not of the most general principles, but of nearly all the elements of the Kabbalah, in the *Zend Avesta* and the religious commentaries which depend upon it.

Incidentally, this vast and admirable monument, which has been known to us for more than a century, has not yet rendered all the service for the philosophy of history —the true science of the human mind—which we have a right to expect. We do not pretend to fill the gaps in our knowledge of the history of philosophy; but we hope to demonstrate the transmission of ideas between Persia and Judea, as we have already done with reference to Judea and Alexandria.

We must first point out that all chronologists, whether Jewish or Christian, agree that the first liberation of the Israelites who had been captives in Chaldea during the time of Nebuchadnezzar (Ezra 1: 1) took place during the early years of the reign of Cyrus over Babylon, 536 to 530 before the Christian era. If we are to believe the calculations of Anquetil-Dupperon, Zoroaster had already commenced his religious mission in 549—that is, at least fourteen years before the first return of the captive Hebrews to their fatherland. Zoroaster was then forty years old; the most brilliant epoch of his life had begun, and it continued until 539. During these ten years, he converted the entire court and kingdom of King Gustasp, believed to have been Hystaspis, father of Darius. During the same period, the reputation of the new prophet alarmed even the Brahmins of India, and when one of them came to Gustasp's court to overpower what he called an impostor, he and his entourage were compelled to yield to the irresistible power of their adversary. From 539 to 524, Zoroaster openly taught his religion in the capital of the Babylonian empire, which he converted entirely by prudently combining his own doctrines with existing traditions.

Is it reasonable to suppose that the Israelites, who witnessed and must have been indelibly impressed with such a revolution, returning to their fatherland when it was at its height, carried away no trace of it, even in their most secret opinions and ideas? The great question of the origin of evil, until then untouched by Judaism, is, so to speak, the center and starting point of the Persian religion.

Must it not have acted powerfully on the imagination of these people of the Orient, accustomed to explain everything by divine intervention? It cannot be argued that, crushed under the weight of their misfortune, the Hebrews remained indifferent to events in the land of their exile. The Scriptures themselves point with some satisfaction to the Hebrew captives' instruction in all the sciences and, consequently, ideas of their conquerors, which admitted them to the highest offices of the empire.

This was precisely the case with Daniel, Zerubabel and Nehemiah, the latter two of whom played such an active part in the deliverance of their brethren. This is not all. Forty thousand returned to Jerusalem under Zerubabel; a second emigration, headed by Ezra, took place under reign of Artaxerxes Longimanus, about seventy years after the first one. During this interval the religious reform of Zoroaster had time to spread to all parts of the Babylonian empire and to take deep root in the minds of the people. From their return to Palestine until their conquest by Alexander the Great, the Jews remained subject to the Persian kings. And even after the conquest, until their total dispersion, they seem to have looked upon the Euphrates, whose banks they once bathed with their tears, as their second fatherland. The Babylonian synagogue arose under the civil and religious hegemony of the Leaders of the Captivity, and it cooperated with the synagogue in Palestine towards the definite organization of rabbinic Judaism.

Wherever they found an asylum—at Sura, at Pompadita and at Nehardea—they founded religious schools which flourished no less than those of the metropolis. Among the teachers who sprang from their midst, we mention Hillel the Babylonian, who died about forty years before the advent of Christ; Hillel was the teacher of Yohanan ben Zakai, who played such a big part in the kabbalistic stories. The same schools produced the Babylonian Talmud, the final and most complete expression of Judaism. We may conclude that no nation exerted so deep an influence on the Jews as the Persians; that no moral power could have penetrated more deeply into their spirit than did the religious system of Zoroaster with its long procession of traditions and commentaries.

But all doubt vanishes when we pass from the purely external relations between the two nations to a comparison of the ideas which represent the loftiest conclusions and the very foundations of their respective civilizations. Let us cite a few examples of the influence of the Persian religion upon Judaism in general, before pointing out all the elements of the kabbalistic system to be found in the *Zend Avesta.* However, I do not intend to speak of the fundamental dogmas of the Old Testament. For, since Zoroaster himself continually refers to much older traditions, it would be incorrect to regard the following as having been borrowed from his doctrine: the six days of the Creation, so easily recognized in the six Gahanbars; the earthly paradise and the ruse of the demon who, in the shape of a serpent, kindled revolt in the soul of our primal parents; the terrible punishment and forfeiture Adam and Eve had to suffer for this sin (after having lived like angels, they were obliged to cover themselves with the skins of animals, to wrest metals from the bowels of the earth and to invent all the arts by which we subsist); and finally, the last judgment, with its accompanying terrors, and the resurrection of the spirit and the flesh. All these beliefs, it is true, are as explicitly stated in the *Bundehesh* (according to *Zend Avesta,* the oldest religious book of the Parsees) and in the *Zend Avesta* as in Genesis; but we reassert our conviction that the source is to be looked for in a much earlier age. We cannot say the same of rabbinical Judaism, which is much more modern than the religion of Zoroaster. The traces of Parseeism are very visible, and the oldest masters of Kabbalah are also counted among the teachers of the Mishna and the most venerated elders of the synagogue.

Ormuzd himself tells his servant Zoroaster that he, Ormuzd, has given (or created) a place of delight and abundance, called *Eeriene Veedjo*. This place, more beautiful than the entire world, resembles the *Behesht* (the celestial paradise). Ahriman then created in the river that watered this place the Great Adder, mother of winter. (*Zend Avesta Vendidad*, Vol. II, p. 264.) At another point Ahriman himself descends from heaven to earth in the shape of an adder. It is also Ahriman who seduces the first man, *Meshiah*, and the first woman, *Meshiane*. "He crept over their thoughts, he overthrew their minds, and said to them: 'It was Ahriman who made the water, the earth, the trees and the animals.' Thus Ahriman deceived them at the very beginning, and until the end this cruel one endeavored to seduce them."—*Zend Avesta*, Vol. III, pp. 351 and 378.

Side by side with the wisest maxims on the ways of life, and the most consoling thoughts on mercy and divine justice, we find in Judaism traces of the darkest superstition; we must look for their source in the terror instilled by demonology. So great is the power ascribed to the evil spirits that at every moment of his life man may think himself surrounded by invisible enemies set upon taking his soul as well as his body. Even before man is born, they await him at the cradle to contend with God and the tenderness of a mother for him. No sooner does he open his eyes upon this world than they assail his head with a thousand perils and his thoughts with a thousand impure visions. Then, woe to him if he does not always resist! For, before life has entirely departed the body, the evil spirits come to take possession of their prey.

Now in all such ideas there is a perfect similarity between the Jewish traditions and the *Zend Avesta.* According to the latter, the demons or devils, those children of Ahriman and darkness, are as numerous as the creatures of Ormuzd. There are more than a thousand species that present themselves in all manner of form and wander the earth spreading disease and sickness among men. "Where," asks Zoroaster of Ormuzd, "is the site of the male or the female devils? Where do the devils roam in mobs of fifty, a hundred, a thousand, ten thousand, and, finally, all over the place? . . . Destroy the devils that enfeeble men and those that produce sickness, who carry off man's heart as the wind sweeps away the clouds." This is how the Talmud expresses itself on the same subject:

> Abba Benjamin said: 'No creature could withstand the evil spirits if the eye had the capacity to see them.' Abbaye adds: 'They are more numerous than we, and surround us as a ditch surrounds a field.'

> 'Every one of us,' says Rab Hunna, 'has a thousand of them on the left and ten thousand on the right. When we feel ourselves pressed in a crowd, it is because of their presence; when our knees give way under our body, they alone are the cause; when we feel as if our limbs have been broken, it is to them we must attribute this suffering.'

"The devils," says the *Zend Avesta*, "unite with one another and reproduce in the manner of men." (*Zend Av.*, Vol. II, p. 336.) But they also reproduce through our impurities, through the disgraceful acts of self-abuse, and even through the involuntary licentiousness provoked by a voluptuous thought during sleep. According to the Talmud, the demons resemble the angels in three respects, and in three other respects they resemble man. Like the angels they read the future, have wings and fly in a moment from one end of the world to the other; but they eat, drink and reproduce as man does. Furthermore, they all had their origin in the lascivious dreams that troubled the nights of our father during the years passed in solitude, and even today, the same cause produces the same effect in his descendants. Whence the prayers, formulated by Jews and Parsees, to avoid this misfortune. Finally, the same phantoms, the same terrors, besiege both Jew and Parsee at his last moment.

Man is scarcely dead, say the *Zend* books, when he is possessed and questioned by the demons. The Daroudj (the demon) Nesosh comes in the form of a fly, alights upon the head and beats him mercilessly. The soul, separated from the body, arrives at the bridge Chinevad, which separates our world from the invisible world; there it is judged by two angels, one of whom is Mithra, of colossal proportions, with ten thousand eyes and holding a club in his hand.

The rabbis, retaining the same basic idea, render it even more frightful.

> When a man who is about to leave this world opens his eyes, he notices an extraordinary light in his room; standing before him he sees the angel of the Lord,

> clothed in light, his body studded with eyes and his hand holding a flaming sword. At this sight the dying man is seized with a fright that fills his body and spirit. His soul flies from limb to limb, like a man who would shift places. But seeing that it is impossible to escape, he looks the one before him straight in the face and delivers himself entirely into his power. If the dying man is righteous, the divine presence (Shekinah) appears before him and the soul immediately flies far away from the body.

This first test is followed by another, called the torture or the ordeal of the grave. According to the Kabbalists, there are seven ordeals: (1) the separation of body and soul; (2) the recapitulation of the deeds of our life; (3) the time of burial; (4) the ordeal or judgment of the grave; (5) the time when the dead, still animated by the vital spirit, feels the biting of the worms; (6) the punishment of hell; (7) the metempsychosis.

> No sooner is the dead man interred in the grave than the soul unites with him again and, opening his eyes, he sees two angels come to judge him. Each holds in his hand two fiery rods (others say, fiery chains), and the soul and body are simultaneously judged for the evil they have done together. Woe to the man who is found guilty, for no one will defend him! At the first blow, all his limbs are dislocated; at the second, all his bones are broken. But his body is immediately reconstructed and punishment begins anew.

We should value these traditions all the more as they have been taken almost literally from the *Zohar*, whence they passed into purely rabbinical writings and popular collections. We can add to these beliefs a host of religious customs and practices, prescribed by both the Talmud and the *Zend Avesta.* Thus the Parsee, on leaving his bed in the morning, may not take four steps without first girdling his loins with the sacred belt which is called the Kosti. Under the pretext that during the night he has been contaminated by contact with demons, he may not touch any part of his body before washing his hands and face three times. We find the same duties, based on the same reasons, practiced by the followers of rabbinical law, except that the Kosti is replaced by a garment of another shape. Both the disciples of Zoroaster and the followers of the Talmud consider themselves duty bound to greet the moon at its first quarter with prayers and thanksgivings. The practices of defending the dead and the newborn from the demons who try to possess them are nearly the same in both religions. When a Parsee woman has been delivered of a child, a burning lamp or a fire is maintained in her room for three days and three nights. The Jews observe the same custom at death. The ceremony of keeping away the demon Lillith from the newborn is still more complicated. But the reason for it and a description of it are given in the book of Raziel.

The Parsee as well as the Jew carries his devotion even to profanation. There are prayers and religious duties for every moment, for every action, for every situation of the physical and moral life. Although we do not lack material for further expansion on this subject, we think it time to terminate this parallel. But even the fantastic and eccentric facts which we have cited lend greater certainty to our conclusion. For it is surely not in such beliefs and actions that we can invoke the general laws of the human mind. We have demonstrated that the religion—that is to say, the civilization of ancient Persia—left numerous traces in all parts of Judaism: in its celestial mythology, represented by the angels; in its infernal mythology; and, finally, in the religious practices. Shall we believe that its philosophy—that is, the Kabbalah—alone escaped this influence, when we know that the kabbalistic tradition developed in the same manner and at the same time as the oral Law of the talmudic tradition and relies upon the same names? Far be it from us to content ourselves with a simple conjecture, no matter how well founded, on so grave a subject. We shall take up, one by one, all the essential elements of the Kabbalah and show their resemblance to the metaphysical principles of the religion of Zoroaster.

1. The part filled in the Kabbalah by the Ayn Sof, the infinite without name and without form, is assigned in the theology of the Magi to eternal time (Zervane Akerene) and, according to others, to limitless space. Let us note that the term "space" or "absolute place" has become with the Hebrews the very name of the Divinity. Furthermore, this first principle, the unique and supreme source of all existence, is only an abstract God, Who does not act directly on His creatures or relates actively to the world and consequently has no appreciable form we can see; for good as well as evil, light as well as darkness, are together in His bosom. According to the sect of the Zervanites, whose theory has been preserved by Sharistani, a Persian historian, Zervan himself, like the crown of the Kabbalists, is the first emanation of infinite light.

2. The *Memra* of the Chaldean translators is easily recognized in the following words by which Ormuzd himself defines the *Honover* or the creative word:

> The pure, the holy, the sagacious Honover, I tell you, O wise Zoroaster! existed before the heavens, before the

> waters, before the earth, before the herds, before the trees, before the fire, son of Ormuzd, before the pure man, before the devils, before the whole extant world, before all virtues.

By the same word Ormuzd created the world, and by it he acts and exists. Not only did the word antedate the world but, although "given by God," as the *Zend* books say, it is as eternal as He is. It takes the part of mediator between limitless time and the existences that flow from its bosom. It embraces the source and model of all perfection and has the power to realize them in all beings. Finally, what establishes its resemblance with the kabbalistic word is that it has a body and a spirit—that is to say, it is Spirit and Word at the same time. It is the Spirit because it is nothing less than the soul of Ormuzd, as he himself expressly says; it is the Word or body—that is to say, spirit become visible—because it is at one and the same time the law and the universe.

3. In Ormuzd we find something that fully resembles what the *Zohar* calls a "person" or "face." Ormuzd is, in fact, the highest personification of the creative word, of that "excellent word" of which his soul is made. It is in him also, rather than in the supreme principle, in eternal time, that we should look for the union of all the characteristics ordinarily attributed to God, and of which he is the manifestation, or, in the language of the Orient, the most brilliant and purest light. "In the beginning," say the sacred books of the Parsees, "Ormuzd, elevated above everything, was with sovereign learning and purity in the light of the world. This luminous throne, this place where Ormuzd dwelled, is called the prime light." Like the celestial man of the Kabbalists, he combines in him-

self true knowledge, the highest degree of intelligence, greatness, goodness, beauty, energy or strength, purity or splendor; finally, it is he who created, or at least formed and nourishes, all beings.

There is nothing conclusive, of course, about these qualities themselves or their resemblance to the Sefiroth, but we cannot help noticing that they are all united in Ormuzd, whose role, in relation to infinity, and to unlimited time, is the same as Adam Kadmon's to the Ayn Sof. Indeed, if we are to believe Sharistani, there was a large Persian sect which held that Ormuzd was the divine will manifested in a resplendent human form. True, the *Zend* books do not explain how Ormuzd brought forth the world, how he himself as well as his enemy emerged from the bosom of the Eternal, and what constitutes the prime substance of things. But when God is compared to light, the efficient cause of the world subordinated to a higher principle, the universe considered as the body of the invisible word, we cannot help looking upon beings as isolated words of this eternal word or as the rays of this infinite light. Also, Gnostic pantheism is more or less connected with the fundamental principle of the theology of the Parsees.

It is nevertheless important to note that in the *Zend Avesta,* Ormuzd is called the "body of bodies." Is this not, perhaps, the substance of substances, the basis of the Kabbalists? Burnouf mentions also a very old Phelvic commentary where, as in the *Sefer Yetzirah* and the *Zohar,* both worlds are represented by the symbol of a burning coal; the higher world is the flame, and visible nature is the burning matter.

4. According to the kabbalistic belief, as well as the Platonic system, all the beings of this world first existed

in a more perfect form in the invisible world. In divine thought is the invariable model of each thought, which can make its appearance here below only through the imperfection of matter. This conception, where the dogma of pre-existence is confused with the principle of the theory of ideas, is called "Ferouer" in the *Zend Avesta*. The great Orientalist Burnouf explains this word as follows:

> By 'Ferouer,' the Persians understood the divine prototype of each intelligently endowed thing, its idea in the thought of Ormuzd, and the higher spirit that breathes in it and watches over it. This meaning is supported by the tradition as well as by the texts.

We shall not cite all the passages of the *Zend Avesta* that confirm this interpretation. We prefer to point out a very remarkable coincidence between the Kabbalists and the disciples of Zoroaster on one particular point of this doctrine. Recall the magnificent passage in the *Zohar* where the souls, about to be sent to earth, represent to God how they will suffer while away from him; what misery and contamination await them in our world. In the religious traditions of the Parsees the Ferouers make the same complaint, and Ormuzd replies in almost the way as Jehovah answered the souls who were grieved at leaving heaven. He tells them that they were born for struggle, to combat evil and expel it from creation, that they can enjoy immortality and heaven only when their task on earth is accomplished.

> How you will benefit from the fact that, in the world, I shall permit you to exist in bodies! Fight! Sweep away the children of Ahriman! In the end I shall rehabilitate

> you in your first estate and you will be happy. In the end I shall place you again in the world, and you will be immortal, ever young and sound.

Another characteristic that reminds us of the kabbalistic ideas is that nations like individuals have Ferouers: thus the *Zend Avesta* often invokes the Ferouer of Iran, the country where the law of Zoroaster was first recognized. Moreover, this belief, which we also meet in the prophecies of Daniel (10: 10ff), was probably widespread among the Chaldeans long before their political and religious fusion with the Persians.

5. If there is some resemblance between the psychology of the Kabbalists and that of Plato, there is even more between it and that of the Parsees, as represented in a collection of very old traditions reproduced by Auquetil-Duperron in the *Mémoires de l'Académie des Inscriptions.* According to the kabbalistic theories the human soul has three powers, perfectly distinct one from another, which are united only during earthly life. On the highest level is the spirit proper, the pure emanation of Divine Intelligence, destined to return to its source and unaffected by earthly contamination; on the lowest level, immediately above matter, is the principle of motion and sensation, the vital spirit whose task ends at the brink of the grave. Placed between these two extremes, finally, is the seat of good and of evil, the free and responsible principle, the moral person.

Several Kabbalists and some philosophers of great authority in Judaism have added two other principal elements to these three. One of them is the vital principle, distinguished from the principle of sensation, the intermediary power between soul and body; the other is the archetype, or, we may say, the idea, which expresses the articulated form of the individual. This form descends from heaven into woman's womb at the time of conception and departs thirty days before death. During this thirty-day period it is replaced by a shapeless shadow.

The theological traditions of the Parsees set up precisely the same distinctions in the human soul. We easily recognize the individual type in the Ferouer which, having existed in heaven in a pure and isolated state, is compelled, as we have seen, to unite with the body. The vital principle is usually apparent in the Dian, whose role is to conserve the powers of the body and to maintain harmony in all its parts. Like the "He-yah" of the Jews, the Dian takes no part in man's evil; it is but a light vapor that comes from the heart and must merge with the earth after death. The Akko, on the contrary, is the loftiest principle. It is above evil, a kind of light that comes from heaven and must return thither when our body is returned to dust. The Akko is the pure intelligence of Plato and of the Kabbalists, but restricted to knowledge of our duties and the prevision of future life and the resurrection —in short, to moral consciousness.

We finally come to the soul proper or the moral person, which is one, notwithstanding the diversity of its faculties; it alone is responsible to divine judgment for our actions. Another distinction, much less philosophical but equally acknowledged by the *Zend* books, makes man the image of the world, recognizing in his consciousness two opposite principles, two Kedras; one, coming from heaven, leads us to good, while the other, created by Ahriman, tempts us to evil. These two principles leave man liberty of action; they play a prominent role in the Talmud where they become good and evil desire; possibly they also mean the good and evil angel.

6. Even Ahriman's conception, notwithstanding its mythological character, was preserved in the doctrines of the Kabbalah; for darkness and evil are personified in Samael, just as divine light is represented in all its splendor by heavenly man. As for the metaphysical interpretation of this symbol (that the evil principle is matter or, as the Kabbalists say, the "shell," the last degree of existence), it is found, in the sect of the Zerdustians, who established the same relation between divine light and the kingdom of darkness as between a body and its shadow.

But there is another fact, more noteworthy, because it is unique. We find in the oldest parts of the religious codes of the Parsees the kabbalistic view that the Prince of Darkness, Samael, losing half his name, will become an angel of light at the end of time and, together with all who were cursed, return to divine grace. A passage in the *Yacna* reads: "This unjust, impure, gloomy king, who understands only evil, will say Avesta at the resurrection, and, fulfilling the law, will establish it even in the dwelling of the damned (the darwands)." The *Bundehesh* adds that then Ormuzd and the seven prime genii will be seen on one side and Ahriman with an equal number of evil spirits on the other side, together offering a sacrifice to the Eternal, Zervane Akerene. Finally, all these metaphysical and religious ideas are accomplished by a quite peculiar geographical system, which is found with slight variations in both the *Zohar* and the sacred books of the Parsees. According to the *Zend Avesta* and the *Bundehesh,* the earth is divided into seven parts (keshvars), which are watered by seven great rivers and separated from one another by the "water spilled in the beginning." Each part forms a world apart and supports inhabitants of a different nature; some are black, some white; some have bodies covered with hair like animals, others are distinguished by other more or less fantastic configurations. Only one of the large divisions of the earth received the law of Zoroaster.

Here now is the opinion of the Kabbalists on the same subject:

> When God created the world, He stretched above us seven heavens and formed beneath our feet as many lands. He made seven rivers, and established a week of seven days. Each of these heavens has its separate constellation and angels of a particular nature; the same is true of the lands here below. Placed one above the other, they are all inhabited, but by beings of different nature, as are the heavens. Some of the beings have two faces, some four, and others but one. They differ in color too; some are red, some black, and some white. Some have clothes, others are naked as worms. If the objection be raised that all of the world's inhabitants descend from Adam, we ask if it is possible that Adam traveled through all these regions for the purpose of populating them? How many wives did he have? But Adam lived only in that part of the earth which is the most elevated and which is enveloped by the higher heaven.

The only difference between this description and that of the Parsees is that instead of considering the seven parts of the earth as natural divisions of the same surface, the Kabbalists represent them as enveloped one in another, like the layers of an onion.

Such, simply presented and in elementary form, are the elements that constitute the common foundation of the Kabbalah and the religious ideas produced under the influence of the *Zend Avesta.* We would nonetheless retreat from the inevitable deduction if we had not found all the heavenly and infernal mythology, part of the liturgy, and even some of the most essential dogmas of Judaism in the sacred books of the Parsees, as well. Nevertheless, we are far from accusing the Kabbalists of having been but servile imitators; of having adopted strange ideas and beliefs without examination or, at least, without modification; or of having confined themselves to cloaking their ideas with the authority of their own sacred books.

As a general rule there is no instance of a nation, no matter how strong the pressure of another people, giving up its true life, which is the exercise of its inner capacities, for a borrowed life and a borrowed soul. We cannot possibly consider the Kabbalah an isolated fact, accidental in Judaism; on the contrary, it is its heart and soul. For, while the Talmud took over all that relates to the outward practice and performance of the Law, the Kabbalah reserved for itself the domain of speculation and the most formidable problems of natural and revealed theology. It was able, besides, to arouse the veneration of the people by showing inviolate respect for their crude beliefs and teaching them to understand that their entire faith and religion rested upon a sublime mystery. It could do this without resort to artifice by carrying the principle of the allegorical method to its final conclusion.

We have seen in what esteem the Kabbalah was held by the Talmud and what influence it exerted upon the popular imagination. The sentiments it once instilled have come down to fairly modern times, for it was on the kabbalistic ideas that the modern Bar Kochba, Sabbatai Zevi, relied when, for a moment, he unsettled all the Jews of the world. The same ideas caused the liveliest commotion among the Jews of Hungary and Poland towards the close of the eighteenth century, giving birth to the sect of the Zoharites and Neo-Hassidim, and leading thousands of Jews into the bosom of Christianity. Considering the Kabbalah, per se, we cannot help seeing it as an immense advance over the theology of the *Zend Avesta.* True, dualism is the cornerstone of the Zoroastrian structure, but it is not as absolute as is commonly thought, and it is part of a religion which acknowledges one Supreme Being. Ormuzd and Ahriman alone exist in reality, with a divine character and with real power; while the Eternal, that limitless time from which both of them sprang, is, as we said, a pure abstraction. To relieve the Eternal of the responsibility for evil, the management of the world was taken from Him and, consequently, all participation in good; nothing was left to Him but a name with a shadow of existence. But this is not all. In the *Zend Avesta,* as in the later traditions stemming from it, all ideas relating to the invisible world, all the great principles of the human mind, are again wrapped in a mythological veil through which they appear as visible realities and distinct persons made in the image of man.

The doctrine of the Kabbalists presents quite a different character. Here monotheism is the foundation, the basis and the principle of all things; dualism and all other distinctions are only formal. God alone, God One and Supreme, is at once the cause, the substance and the intelligible essence—the ideal form of all that is. Only between being and nothingness, between the highest form and the lowest degree of existence, is there an opposition, a dualism. One is light, the other is darkness. Darkness, therefore, is but a negation; light is the spiritual principle, the eternal wisdom, the infinite intelligence which creates all that it conceives, and conceives or thinks by its very existence. But if this be so, if it be true that at a certain level being and thought blend, the great conceptions of intelligence cannot exist in the mind alone. They do not represent mere forms from which abstractions are made at will; on the contrary, they have a substantive and absolute value—that is to say, they are inseparable from the eternal substance. This is precisely the character of the Sefiroth, of the Heavenly Man, of the Great and Small Face—in short, of all the kabbalistic personifications, which are much different, as can be seen, from the individual and mythological personifications of the *Zend Avesta*.

Still, the outline, the exterior design of the *Zend Avesta*, remained. But the nature of the base was completely altered, and the Kabbalah offers, by the very fact of its birth, the peculiar spectacle of a mythology passing into metaphysics under the very influence of religious sentiment. However, the system which was the fruit of that movement, notwithstanding its scope and depth, is not a work where human reason makes free use of its rights and powers. Mysticism, per se, does not appear in the Kabbalah in its most elevated form, for it still remains chained to an external power—the revealed word. No doubt this power is more apparent than real; no doubt allegory soon made the sacred letter a docile instrument at the service of the mind and its most liberal inspirations. But it cannot be denied that this kind of procedure—whether deliberate or misguided—this art of sheltering new ideas under some secular text, sanctions fatal prejudice against true philosophy. Thus it is that the Kabbalah, although it arose under the influence of a foreign civilization and notwithstanding the pantheism that underlies all its doctrine, retains a Jewish religious and national character.

By taking refuge first in the authority of the Bible and then in the oral Law, it retained all the features of a Jewish theological system. Before it could be admitted into the history of philosophy and humanity, those features had to be wiped out and the Kabbalah shown in its true light—that is to say, as a natural product of the human mind. This obliteration was accomplished, as we have said, slowly but surely, in the capital of the Ptolemies. There, for the first time, the Hebrew traditions stepped over the threshold of the sanctuary and, mingling with many new ideas without loss of their own substance, spread into the world. Wishing to recover a possession they considered their own, the guardians of these traditions welcomed the most noble results of Greek philosophy, combining them more and more with their own beliefs. The pretended heirs to Greek civilization, on the other hand, becoming gradually accustomed to this combination, thought only of bringing the new amalgam into an organized system where Reason and Intuition, Philosophy and Theology, would be equally represented. Thus it was that the Alexandrian school developed a brilliant and profound summary of all the philosophical and religious ideas of antiquity. This explains the resemblance—the identity—between all the essential points of Neo-Platonism and the Kabbalah. But the Kabbalah, though Hellenized, was nevertheless transmitted among the Jews of Palestine in a small circle of the elite and was considered the secret of Israel. In this form it was introduced into Europe and taught until the publication of the *Zohar*.

Here begins a new order of research, viz.: What influence did the Kabbalah exert upon the hermetic and mystic philosophy that attracted such attention from the beginning of the fifteenth to the end of the seventeenth century (Raymond Lullus may be considered its first, and Francis Mercurius van Helmont, its last representative)? This may be the subject of a second work to complement this one. To recapitulate:

1. The Kabbalah is not an imitation of the Platonic philosophy, for Plato was unknown in Palestine, where the kabbalistic system was founded. Furthermore, notwithstanding several points of resemblance which strike us at first glance, the two doctrines differ totally in their most important features.

2. The Kabbalah is not an imitation of the Alexandrian school. First, because it antedates the Alexandrian school, and second, because Judaism has always shown a profound aversion to and ignorance of Greek civilization, even when it placed the Kabbalah in the rank of divine revelation.

3. The Kabbalah cannot be regarded as the work of Philo, although the doctrines of the philosophical theologian contain a great number of kabbalistic ideas. Philo could not have transmitted these ideas to his Palestinian compatriots without at the same time introducing them into Greek philosophy. Given the nature of his mind, Philo was not capable of founding a new doctrine. What is more, it is impossible to find in the monuments of Judaism the least trace of his influence. Finally, Philo's writings are of more recent date than the kabbalistic principles, found in the Septuagint, in the Proverbs of

Jesus ben Sirach, and in the Book of Wisdom.

4. The Kabbalah has not been borrowed from Christianity, for all the great principles upon which it stands antedate the coming of Christ.

5. The striking resemblances which we have found between this doctrine and the religious beliefs of the several sects of Persia, its numerous and remarkable points of similarity with the *Zend Avesta,* the traces that the religion of Zoroaster has left in all parts of Judaism, and the external relations between the Hebrews and their old teachers after the Babylonian captivity—all these force us to the conclusion that the material of the Kabbalah derived from the theology of the ancient Persians. But this borrowing did not destroy the originality of the Kabbalah for the latter substituted the absolute unity of cause and substance for the dualism in God and nature. Instead of explaining the formation of beings as an arbitrary act of inimical forces, it presents them as divine forms, successive and providential manifestations of the Infinite Intelligence. Ideas take the place of realized personifications and mythology is supplanted by metaphysics. This seems to us to be the general law of the human mind. No absolute originality, but also no servile imitation between nations and centuries. Whatever we may do to gain unlimited independence in the domain of moral science, the chain of tradition will always be evident in our boldest discoveries. No matter how immobile we sometimes appear to be under the sway of tradition and authority, our intelligence paves the way, our ideas change with the very power that weighs them down, and a revolution is bound to break loose.